How To Plan Meetings

By Joseph G. Glass, PH.B., LL,B.

www.sunvillagepublications.com

How To Plan Meetings
By Joseph G. Glass, PH.B., LL,B.

Copyright © 2011

No part of this publication may be reproduced, stored in a retrieval system or transmitted in any form or by any means, electronic, mechanical, photocopying, recording or otherwise, without prior written permission from the publisher.

www.sunvillagepublications.com

Cover design by www.WebCopyAlchemy.com

TO

HILDA

LILA

AND

WILLIAM

PREFACE

Democracy has been described as "a constitutional form of government with a system of checks and balances, parliamentary assembly, popular suffrage, periodic elections, and a Bill of Rights. It is based upon respect for the individual and, while adhering to the principle of majority rule as a fundamental tenet of democracy, the rights of minorities to full privileges of citizenship are not abridged under this form of government. It is the aim of Democracy to give the fullest measure of freedom to the individual to develop his maximum capacities so long as this development does not interfere with the welfare and rights of others." But, when this has been said, an essential element of Democracy has been omitted. It's all right as far as it goes; and to some people, it would serve as a reasonably satisfactory definition. Missing in this definition is what I would consider the most necessary element for a successful Democracy.

A fundamental assumption of Democracy is a system of universal education and the dissemination of unbiased news and information *on a basis which will permit of an honestly informed public opinion.* The italicized phrase is the key to a successful Democracy. Freedom, it should be remembered, is the most dangerous thing in the world, for implicit in freedom is the right to make the wrong choice. If we cannot produce a democratic system of government, which enables its people to find sound answers to their problems, to make wise decisions, then our American Democracy cannot endure. For Democracy is, at best, a clumsy, slow-moving method by which men arrive at decisions. Why, then, are we so neglectful in developing techniques that enable us to reach sound conclusions about the enormous problems we face as a free people?

When we lost the early New England Town Meeting,

we lost something precious and extremely valuable to our way of life. We grew so rapidly and great wealth came to us so quickly, we turned to the most hazardous methods of dealing with our common problems: the political rally or mass meeting. Through these meetings, people of congenial minds and attitudes met together to intensify their prejudices, beliefs, and inclinations and—this is equally important—to vilify the ideas and inclinations of those who hold opposing views. Adolph Hitler said of mass meetings: "I require that all my people attend mass meetings . . . What they hear in mass meetings, remains with them ineradicable and impervious to every reasonable explanation."

Mr. Joseph G. Glass, in writing this book, has performed a distinct service to the preservation of American Democracy. He is setting forth in this volume practical answers to a question that is in the minds of millions of Americans today: "How can we develop techniques that will enable us to find the right answers to the grave problems we face?" It is clear that Mr. Glass has had a great deal of first-hand experience in organizing and conducting a wide variety of meetings, the essential purpose of which is to help people arrive at sound conclusions about their common problems. In the days and years ahead we shall find increasing need for the practice of orderly discussion by all of our people. A former president of the United States has wisely said, "There is a proper urge in all Americans for unity in troubled times. But unless unity is based on right principles and right action it is a vain and dangerous thing. Honest difference of views and honest debate are not disunity. They are the vital process of policy-making among free men."

I heartily congratulate Mr. Glass on his service to the American people in writing this book.

GEORGE V. DENNY, JR.

CONTENTS

Chapter 1

IN THE BEGINNING

JUST PULL UP your old armchair and make yourself at home. We are going to have a little discussion about the art of organizing and running a meeting—any kind of a meeting. This is your living room, so why not be comfortable and completely relaxed?

Meetings are called for a variety of reasons. Usually meetings are called for the purpose of exchanging ideas. In the course of progress, human beings have learned that it is to their mutual advantage to get together and tell each other all about new or old discoveries. This is done in the lecture-form called "the class-room," "the mass meeting," "the forum," or in a number of other ways. Another reason for calling meetings is to express an attitude of either approval or disapproval of a given situation.

Human beings are ordinarily interested in the affairs of their community. (At least we hope they are.) When a given situation arises, feelings may be running high one way or the other. Civilized people do not let their emotions control their reactions, and so instead of going out and killing the politician who has been accumulating ill-gotten gain in a tin box, a protest meeting is called for the purpose of inducing the mayor to remove the said politician, or for the purpose of building up sufficient public sentiment to compel the rascal's resignation.

Meetings are also held for patriotic reasons. In times of crisis and in times of peace, it is good to have citizens of a country foregather and express their feeling of pleasure over the fact that they are citizens of this or that country. The patriotic meeting is not necessarily a nationalistic affair. True patriots are always ready to share the blessings of their country with all mankind. We shall not here undertake to outline all the reasons why meetings are held. The examples given are sufficient to clarify the point.

It is all as simple as rolling off a log, and by the time we are through, we are going to look forward to the meetings we used to dread.

It is regrettable that all meetings are not stimulating or even enjoyable. Many times meetings are just plain boring. There is no reason why a meeting should be boring. If it is well planned and the efforts put forth are properly channelized, the result must be a good one. For example, in a well-planned meeting, the ability of the speaker to hold the audience's attention is known in advance. We do not arrange a meeting in a hit-or-miss fashion. It is done according to a carefully laid-out plan. When, therefore, meetings are stimulating and interesting instead of being boring and repelling, the likelihood is that the organization undertaking to run meetings regularly will find a steady and responsive following.

AW through this book we are going to pretend that we are talking to each other or among ourselves as a group. It will depend upon the situation at hand. "We" is defined as you the reader, and "I" the author, or "you" the readers and "I" the author.

In order to understand fully what we have to do and how to do it, we should discuss first things first, and so, without any further ado, we shall begin to talk about the kinds of

(12)

meetings we may have. Let us divide them into arbitrary categories and *give* each category a thorough going-over.

Here is a list of meetings most of us know something about:

1. The lecture—one subject, one speaker
2. The symposium—one subject
3. The forum—political—science—business
4. The debate—one subject
5. The round-table or informal discussion
6. The mass meeting—one specific purpose and subject

Why are meetings called ?

(a)   To protest against something
(b)   To agitate for something
(c)   To spread information
(d)   To attempt organization for or against a given situation

First, let us talk about a lecture meeting. This kind of meeting deals with a straight talk. It can be given a lot of fancy names, but a lecture after all is nothing more or less than one human being talking to a lot of others who either want to or must listen to what the speaker has to say.

A lecture may be delivered in one talk or a series of talks —all of them on the same subject.

The one who delivers the lecture is referred to as the lecturer. A lecture sometimes may be divided into a number of talks. This of course is referred to as a lecture series. In most instances, however, the lecture is delivered on a single occasion. Of course, the types of lectures may vary. There is the straight talk by an individual who is supposed to have accumulated a great deal of knowledge about a given subject.

(13)

He simply recites to the listeners that which he feels is of importance and of interest to them. Then we have the illustrated lecture where pictures or sketches or designs of some kind are used to help illustrate the points being made. A third type of lecture is the narrator type. Here we generally find the motion picture being used as an adjunct to the talk. While the picture is being flashed on the screen the lecturer keeps up a running commentary. In addition to the types of lectures just described, there are a number of others. There is nothing to prevent any organization from arranging a lecture in any form or combination of forms that best fits the purposes of the organization in question.

Suppose then that we are going to run a lecture series, or even only one lecture. Any group or organization can have lectures. No special reason or right to do so is necessary.

Many groups are reluctant to undertake the burden of running lectures. This reluctance is based chiefly on the fact that there has been no prior experience. Any organization can run a lecture if it has a meeting place or if it can obtain a meeting place. The only thing is that the organization must be one that stands for a purpose or ideal that attracts the attention of others. The political group or the history society or the botanic garden group or the religious or church group all have need of a good reason to run meetings of one type or another, especially the lecture-type of meeting.

We begin by choosing the *subject* or the topic of the lecture.

The subject is always one that has some relationship to the group or organization. A garden group wants to know more about gardens, lawyers more about daw, doctors more about medicine, and politicians—who knows what ? The sub-

(14)

ject is chosen with the idea in mind that the members or invited guests will find it of interest and want very much to hear what is going to be said.

When that's done, we scout around and try to find the man or woman who is best qualified to *give* the lecture. Always try to get the best in the field.

By the term "the best in the field" is not necessarily meant the big-name individuals. There are many well-known persons in our country and in other parts of the world who are complete bores and are not even entitled to the fame that attaches to their name. Their presence may attract a number of people to a meeting, but the end-result is that the audience will begin to resist invitations to future events. On the other hand, if it is possible to obtain the services of a well-known individual who is not only well known but also competent, then by all means choose such a person as your speaker.

A lecture series that starts with well-known and thoroughly competent individuals can pretty safely go along on its own steam with lesser known but also competent individuals. It is necessary, of course, first to establish a good reputation before attempting to build the lecture series around the lesser lights. If there should happen to be an authority who is an unknown, such authority should be used when the organization's lecture series is at the crest of the wave of popularity. The needs of democracy are great and some of these needs are satisfied by building up unknown individuals who can contribute to the exchange of ideas.

Later on in this book we'll talk about how and where to find lecturers. While we are doing this, we make it our business to arrange for a place and a time where all this will come about. Let us assume we are successful and we have the subject, the person, the place, and the time. This is only

(15)

the beginning. There are a great many other things that must be done. Let's go back for a moment and clear up a few points that we have glossed over very lightly. Running a meeting is a complicated job and requires much time and effort. There are always a thousand and one details that have to be attended to and unless we find a genius with a dozen heads and almost two dozen hands, and a mind capable of thinking of scores of things at one time, we soon become convinced that a committee is what is needed.

In every organization there are many members who just go along with the tide. There are also in every organization a few who are willing to do most or all of the work required. It is unfair to burden these willing souls. They should be assisted by a committee. The unwilling ones should as far as possible be induced or compelled to work along with the very active members. In most clubs or societies members are not paid for the services they render. It is unfair to heap upon them the obligations of all the members. Always bear this fact in mind. Therefore, we come to the conclusion that a successful lecture or series of lectures must be organized and run by a working committee. Get up a committee that will work and take care of details. The average committee has to attend to details that are not surrounded by any glory. The work of the committee is important but inconspicuous. The honors and the praise go to someone else, but the truth is that the honor and praise that someone else gets for the most part really belong to that little group of committee members who see to it or who saw to it that all the details were attended to. The committee is either elected by the members of the organization or appointed by the top officers.

The composition of a committee is very important. Every committee must be composed of people who are interested in the purpose for which the committee has been organized.

Thus a committee that is designated for the purpose of arranging for a lecture or a series of lectures or a meeting of some kind should be composed only of members who agree that it is a good idea to hold such a lecture or series of lectures. Do not have on the committee persons who have any doubts about the value of such work.

The weakest link in the chain of organization is the member who has doubts about the work being done. The halfhearted approach of the doubtful member infects other committee members and causes dissension or lack of cooperative effort. It is better to have more work for each committee member without the doubter, than to hope that he will assist by keeping him on the committee roster.

The committee members should be persons who can get along well. Wherever possible, the committee members should be chosen because each one has an ability to do a good job in a *special* field. For example, if a Mrs. Tooth-feather is known to be an expert on corralling interesting speakers, she should by all means be included in the committee, or if Mrs. Wormturner is known for her ability to write interesting copy for new releases, she too should be included in the committee.

Where a committee is an all-inclusive one, specialists in different fields should be included. Thus a committee should have a member or two capable of writing press releases, another member or two capable of arranging the social part of the evening, and another member or two capable of finding out just where it is possible to *get* the best-informed person in a given field. Sometimes it becomes necessary to form special committees for publicity work, contact work, etc. Where such special committees are set up they should be composed of specialists in that activity.

There are some men and women who are just plain Jim-

17

my and Jenny Higginses. No organization of any kind whatsoever, where unpaid personnel is depended on, can possibly continue to function or exist without these Jimmy and Jenny Higginses. They are the self-effacing individuals who contribute their all because they love the work they are doing. There is no adequate way known yet to express fully the debt of mankind to people of this type and nature. They do all the hard work and get very little of the glory. They are the salt of the earth. By all means they should be included in the committee membership.

It is better for the committee to choose its own chairman than to have a chairman set up a committee. Permitting a committee to choose its own chairman is an other manifestation of democracy in action. In addition, it will put at the head of a committee the person most capable of getting the work done quickly and efficiently. This is the general rule, but not an absolute rule. Many people resent the idea of being compelled to work under another individual's direction or supervision unless they've had a say in choosing the person in charge. That is a natural reaction. A chairman is designated in advance only when he is known to be a person capable of organizing a committee that will be happy to function under his supervision and direction. The chairman must be capable of coordinating all of the activities of the committee. He should be tactful, inspiring, intelligent, and efficient.

Here we are in your living room planning for the lecture that is going to take place on the first Tuesday in October, right after all of our neighbors and citizens in general have returned from their summer vacation. It's going to be one of the big events of the year. We are going to take care of every little detail right now.

(18)

Our committee is in session. Pretend that we are interested in having a lecture on the subject of "The Proper Approach Psychologically to a Young Dog." To dog lovers this is a very important subject, and should attract a lot of people because there are a lot of dogs and dog owners in our town. Very likely it will come as a surprise to some people that there is such a thing as dog psychology. Persons who have spent a good deal of time studying and training dogs assure us that there definitely is such a thing. They maintain that to a very large degree dogs are psychologically influenced just as humans are.

Problem number one: How to word the subject of the lecture. We want to make it sound interesting and exciting so that we can bring out everyone of the persons we believe ought to be present.

Very carefully we begin to choose words to be put into the *title* of the lecture and full notices that are to go out. The title is the first thing that everyone sees and, except for the names of very famous persons, the title is the thing that will most likely decide for the prospective audience-member the question of whether or not to attend. The title must create an instantaneous reaction. You can't depend on the title's being given a second chance to make its full import felt. The words must be plain and full of power. They must build a picture of something interesting. Keep at it until the words are put together in a tricky fashion. Those who see the notices must be impressed with the subject of the lecture. Almost any lecture is of interest to any number of people provided the notice is so presented that it compels their attention and each reader feels he *must* attend. Writing notices is not difficult. It takes time and patience. Swap ideas around. Have the notices read by a number of persons and pay close attention to all suggestions. Some you can throw

(19)

into the waste basket immediately, others you can develop or change. Don't be too anxious to fill up the waste basket. In any event give this phase of your work much time and study.

Someone suggests that we send out a very polite letter to all the persons who have obtained licenses for dogs. That's a good idea—but that's not enough, and besides which, where does one go to find the names of persons who have licenses for their dogs?

To illustrate what we mean we would suggest that a check be made with the local ASPCA, the Board of Health, the Department of Licenses, the local Dog Pound, the County Board, or even the Village Clerk. Every possible avenue should be exploited. We are beginning to get up steam. Mrs. Jones will be the committee member who will contact the Society for the Prevention of Cruelty to Animals and other organizations, and ask them where such names can be obtained. She will get the list and have it ready for our next meeting. Sometimes the lists are confidential and may not be made public. Try and arrange with the keeper of the confidential record to have your mailing list sent to the list of names that are kept in confidence without the list's being divulged to you.

The usual things are easy to do. It requires no great effort and very little imagination. It is the extraordinary things that impress the members of the organization and that frequently bring unexpected results. For example, since we are talking about dogs, why not write to dog food manufacturers and ask them for assistance? This one example is enough to demonstrate the fact that the prospects are almost limitless.

Problem number two: Publicity. There are many people who do not have dogs and may very well be interested in

(20)

what our speaker is going to have to say. "Why not send a notice to all the newspapers?" asks Mrs. Smith. That's a good idea, and so we give Mrs. Smith the job of finding out the addresses of all the newspapers and local blurb sheets that may carry our announcement.

To many people the art of approaching newspapers or magazines seems to border on the mysterious. That, of course, is not the fact at all. To approach a newspaper or magazine editor or anyone else for that matter, the simplest thing to do is just go there convinced that your visit is important enough for the individual in question to see you. Always bear in mind that newspapers and like media are anxious to reach the public, and it is important for them to know what the public is thinking. Have all your ideas and thoughts well organized so that there will be a minimum of delay if, as, and when you are permitted to enter this sanctum sanctorum of the editor. If possible have everything written down either in outline or in completed form. Editors are hard pressed for time. Your reception will always be better when you come well prepared.

All of a sudden, Mrs. Smith, who is now very proud of the fact that something she is going to write will appear in the local newspaper, gets another idea. Why can't we write to Suzie Skinnybones, the morning chatterbox on radio station WWWW, and ask her to talk about our coming lecture, when she tells all the women in town how to make beautiful table mats out of their husband's discarded rubber tires? Miss Skinnybones is always making announcements about events to come. Of course, Mrs. Smith likes the idea of talking to Miss Skinnybones and she, therefore, will be given that additional job.

What is true of the editor is also true of the radio personality. Whenever possible try to make an appointment by

(21)

telephone in advance. The more popular radio newscasters, commentators, etc. have secretaries who are trained to receive the public in a courteous manner. They are approachable if one takes the time to see them when their schedule will permit. Sometimes, of course, it is possible just to pay a visit to a popular personality at a radio or television broadcast without any prior appointment having been made. It may be just your luck to be received and find that you have been given a good break.

Over in the corner is quiet Mrs. Black who doesn't talk very much, but she can be depended on to make a real contribution to the committee's work. Says quiet Mrs. Black in a most apologetic tone, "I saw my boy Jimmie and a number of other boys handing out leaflets at the corner of Main Street announcing the Boy Scout jamboree and cookie sale. The boys were having a wonderful time. So many people stopped and talked with them. Why can't we have our boys distribute the leaflets we print?" Drawing in young people to help as much as possible—the importance and the value of bringing in young people—cannot be overemphasized. The greater the number of young people, the greater the likelihood of successful activity and continuing life for your organization.

There was no objection to Mrs. Black's idea and everyone was enthusiastic about asking their little Johnnies or Jimmies to help out. Things were sure happening fast at this committee meeting. Mrs. Black was put in charge of a number of things. She was going to help write the leaflet that was to be handed out by her boy and some of his friends. More about writing leaflets later. She will see to it that all of them get behind the idea and lend a hand in a real big way. Notice how we are moving along! Democracy makes room for everyone.

(22)

Frequently, a committee member undertakes to do a job that requires the assistance of a subcommittee. A subcommittee can also be called an assistance committee. The subcommittee is always responsible to the parent committee. It is created for the purpose of very carefully carrying out a particular detail of the work in hand. Subcommittees almost always consists of specialists with unusual qualifications. Sometimes subcommittees are the same as special committees just because of this fact. The committee member should be permitted to organize a subcommittee and should be told exactly what work the subcommittee is to do. The committee member in charge of a subcommittee is directly and personally responsible for all the work of the subcommittee.

At this point (we are still in our living room), the chair-lady of the committee on education through lectures feels called upon to make a contribution to the accumulation of ideas on how to gather a goodly crowd. "Of course, you should remember that every one of us has friends and relatives whom we call on the telephone or visit. We should *give* every one of them a personal invitation. That should bring a great many people to our lecture." Everyone agrees with the chairlady and each committee member promises to make a written list of the names and addresses of all friends, relatives, near-friends, and anyone else who could possibly be induced to come, and also to get other members to do likewise.

A written list of this kind is extremely important. It makes it impossible to forget this or that person. It is important not only to the organization but also to the individual who compiles the list. In the course of the compilation, many unrelated facts suddenly come to mind as the member is jotting down the name of a given individual. He suddenly remembers that the following week is the silver anniversary of Aunt Tilly Tish about which he had forgotten and he also remembers that the failure to remember Aunt Tilly Tish would result in a small riot within the family circle. Another member in the course of compiling the list is reminded of the fact that she failed to return the silver cake forks she borrowed from Mrs. Tosh a number of weeks ago. Please remember to turn the lists in. How often have we carried out certain promises to do this or that, and then very promptly forgotten to make the results available to the persons or organizations to whom we made the promise. The best list in the world resting snugly in your jacket pocket or in the bottom of a lady's handbag is of no value to anyone. Personal contact is an important part of the activity relating to building up a successful meeting. Generally speaking, it is safe to say that you can depend on persons whom you invite personally to come to your lecture or meeting. They come either out of obligation to you or because they rely upon your good and discriminating taste.

Each one of us as a general rule enjoys the confidence of friends or relatives, as far as certain matters are concerned. One may be looked upon as a qualified critic of good shows, another may be considered a walking encyclopedia of latest ideas in interior decorating, and still another may have achieved the great goal of knowing all the scandals attached to all the glamorous Hollywood topflight personalities. As a member of an organization with sponsors, lecturers, or meetings of one kind or another, you should be considered by your friends and relatives as an authority on what constitutes a good lecture or lecturer, and your invitation should carry sufficient weight to be almost the equivalent of a command to attend. Note: If you invite a person to attend always be certain to be on hand.

Unless you are prevented by justifiable causes from appearing personally at the meeting, you should be present to receive all those whom you have personally invited. If you do not intend to be present, state so at the very outset. This will avoid creating situations that prove embarrassing and unpleasant. If B agrees to attend a lecture or any other meeting to which he has been invited by A, B is within his rights, when he goes there, to expect to find A present. If A has simply recommended a given meeting to B, then of course A is absolved from the obligation of attending. If you are a member of an organization, and you invite others, make every effort to be present. It helps to build up the permanent audience which your organization is striving for. Be ready to extend your personal greetings at the meeting to the individual or individuals you invited.

Problem number three: By this time, the question of when to have the lecture comes up for consideration. Mrs. Black suggests that, instead of having the lecture on the first Tuesday in October, it be postponed to the third Tuesday in October. She has a good reason for it. Her explanation follows: the annual town bazaar for the Volunteer Fire Department is to be held on the first Friday in October and many people will be actively engaged in helping out. Very likely, they will be tired after all their hard work on behalf of our water-squirting heroes, and furthermore, Mrs. Jones's husband, who is always so helpful, is in charge of the decorations' committee at the bazaar. Yes, the committee must pick another day. The day and date are not chosen blindly. Careful consideration must be given to the important events in the given locality. The season of the year and the possibility of conflict with other events that are known to be in the offing should at all times be avoided. Also remember to give yourself sufficient time to build up the enthusiasm for your meeting. The reason just given is a good one. Avoid conflicts with other events. Try to pick a time when the lecture will be an outstanding event. Of course, this is not always possible, but that fact should be borne in mind.

Remember that what is said here must be modified to suit the particular situation facing the group. In large cities it is not too serious a matter when dates conflict except, of course, a conflict with some event that is the sole topic of conversation. In New Orleans, for example, it would be sheer folly to try bucking up against the Mardi Gras. In Washington, D.C. the day of the inauguration of a new President would be a poor day to pick. The best guide is past experience and good common sense. In smaller cities or town or villages the matter of competing with other events is important. The inhabitants of a small town or city are capable of absorbing only so much activity and no more. Past experience should be able to act as a guide in telling you whether or not the date you have picked will come at a time when the social season is at its height, or when most of the folks in town are busily engaged with the preparation for annual graduation exercises, etc. etc.

You will note, then, that the time when a lecture or meeting is to be held should be very carefully chosen. If any other organization in the same field as your organization is planning a meeting, and there is no reason for you to try to oppose the meeting held by the other organization, then it would be best to try to make arrangements between the two groups. Arrangements between the two groups may include a number of things. One of these is the swapping of lists of names. Every organization, as time goes on, accumulates a list of names. They include members, occasional visitors, interested individuals who are not members, and sundry others. Thus the swapping of the list of names opens the field for you to a new group. Another type of arrangement that can be entered into with another organization is exchange of posters and the placement of notices on each other's bulletin boards. Announcements of coming events at membership meetings can also be taken care of. Maybe you can exchange mailing lists and maybe even the other organization will announce your forthcoming lecture.

The committee decides that the lecture is to be held the third Tuesday in the month. That is the time when a goodly crowd can be expected.

Problem number four: The next question before the committee is where to hold the meeting. The chairlady, Mrs. Pie, suggests that the meeting be held at the Strangefellows Hall. She knows that the auditorium can be obtained for a very small fee. Immediately there are a number of objections. Little Mrs. Black stands up and says, "I do not believe that we should have our lecture at the Strangefellows Hall because the building is an old and gloomy one. There is a constant and penetrating odor of stale smoke and you get the feeling when you enter the place that all the ghosts of yesteryear have come back to haunt the people who disturb their slumber." A number of other committee members agree, "Yes, yes, that's true, that *is* a gloomy place!" Suddenly Mrs. McAstor offers a suggestion, "Why can't we take a nice clean airy room at the Central Hotel. That's conveniently located and besides which the chairs are comfortable. The meeting rooms are so inviting. The bulletin board in the hotel always announces coming events at least one week in advance." Mrs. Bird is in favor of the last suggestion and she adds, "It makes our society appear to be so much richer and more important if we meet at the hotel. People do like to be impressed." That clinches it. The committee agree that they will meet at the Central Hotel because it is conveniently located, the meeting rooms are clean and well ventilated, there is a bulletin board that carries the announcement of the lecture to all those who enter the hotel, the meeting room gives the organization prestige, and it is so much easier for people to remember the place where the lecture is to be held.

It is commonly known that most people react because of deep impressions made upon them. Just plain fact is not sufficient to stimulate them. If your purpose is to attract a group that will attend regularly, then you must bend your efforts and use every trick and device to make a favorable and deep impression. How you impress people differs with each individual. Sometimes you find that a goodly number of persons in the audience are impressed by the fact that they will be required to pay $5.00 per person for admission to see some Hindu fakir perform an inconsequential feat of magic. If the same exhibitions were given free of charge they would not be impressed at all. Some people are impressed by the fact that the meeting is held in a room that has floors which are heavily carpeted. All kinds of things and reasons impress all kinds of people. It is impossible always to satisfy or impress all people. Do the best you can by never *giving* up thinking about how to create impressions. *All these details are important.* They should be borne in mind at all times.

The choice of a place where a lecture or meeting is to be held can sometimes spell the difference between success or dismal failure. Persons who are willing to go to the trouble to attend a meeting or a lecture will do so more readily if they are invited to a place that has some sort of added attraction.

Some kind of urging is always needed to get people to come to your meeting. Find out what type of urging it is that will most likely lead to success and proceed to use just that type. Too often, people who are planning a meeting think only in terms of how much money they can save by using one auditorium or meeting place instead of another. As a general rule the difference in the cost is so small that it is wise to make the additional investment in order to guarantee a successful affair. If, by chance, there is a popular auditorium where meetings are constantly being held, such a place is most desirable. Some places are popular because there is a long and happy tradition attached to them, and some are popular because the audience that goes there is of such a nature that every meeting becomes an interesting event, and some places are popular because of their accessibility. Consider these factors when deciding on an auditorium.

Schools ordinarily are not very popular. There are a number of reasons for this. To many the school is a stiff formal institution where they were subjected in their childhood days to rigid discipline by unapproachable teachers. Old schools have no air conditioning or they are poorly ventilated. In addition, the seats are small and often force us to keep our knees up under our chin. Here and there the school authorities have been able to popularize a given school. When such is the situation, by all means use the school. A popular school is the community center in every case. The community center flourishes in a school that has won the confidence of the people in the particular locality. Not as much effort is necessary to attract people to such a place as to another spot that is also comfortable, accessible, etc. Choose a school in preference to all others whenever you can. Unfortunately, however, this is not always possible. Many organizations conduct meetings in schools. This *is* not always the best place to do so. In most schools, no smoking is allowed. While it is desirable to have a meeting without smoking, in many meetings smoking is permitted. There are many persons who will not attend meetings where they are not permitted to smoke. That, therefore, is an important consideration. Another objection to a school meeting is the fact that in almost all schools the custodian is in a hurry to get the people out. To the custodian, a meeting is just another nuisance. He has to be tipped and the committee never seems to know whether they are tipping enough. Most schools are built for strictly utilitarian purposes. There is usually nothing "warm" about the school auditorium. Some of those who built our schools evidently did so with the idea in mind that a school is little more than a modified form of prison. The school that "feels" like something other than a strait jacket is an exception to the rule. To add to all of the objections above, some people revolt against the idea of going into school because the memories of their school days are not always such memories as they like to recall.

Problem number five: Peace and quiet reign in the living room until the chairlady announces that she favors Professor Higgenbottom as the authority who should be asked to deliver the talk. At this point, a small riot breaks loose. Mrs. Jones, whose mind has been occupied with analyzing the wrong angles of her colleagues' hats, suddenly comes to life. She blurts out, "There are many others who are much more qualified than he is. Last year I heard a lecture by Dr. Toadwart. He is a most interesting speaker. He has a delightful sense of humor, he has written many books and always draws a large crowd. The newspapers quote him constantly and the *Old Ladies Journal* had a series of articles by and about him." By this time a number of the committee members are impressed by the description given to them by Mrs. Jones. Another committee member offers the name of a certain lady whom she heard while visiting some friends last year. There is much talk about the *choice of lecturer* and finally the committee agrees upon Mrs. Jones's candidate. This is an intelligent conclusion.

Whenever a meeting or lecture is being planned, and there is to be only one speaker, that person should be a thoroughly qualified authority in the field. His style of delivery should be attractive and interesting. A sense of humor in a speaker is an individual asset.

Elsewhere in this book we shall try to discuss at great length the subject of humor. Everyone agrees that a sense of humor is an invaluable asset. Just one word, however, about a sense of humor and the use thereof. It is only valuable when the possessor knows how, when, and where to use it.

When it is possible for a chairman to describe the lecturer or speaker as the author of a number of books and articles as well as the gentleman about whom a certain magazine wrote thus and so, and the further fact that the speaker was a member of the Federal Commission of so and so and so and so on, it all adds up to the fact that a good choice has been made. The public notices to the newspapers, the radio, the letters to friends, and the word-of-mouth advertising of the meeting can all build up the importance of the lecturer.

It is now tea time and the chairlady thinks that it would be wise to stop for a moment and see what has been accomplished. She announces the following:

1. We have decided that the time of the lecture is set for the third Friday in October and it will be at 8 P. M.

2. The lecture will be held at the Central Hotel.

3. The lecturer is to be the well-known authority, Dr. Toadwart.

4. Mrs. Black will get up the necessary notices. She will

arrange to have them printed and distributed. Mrs. Smith is going to contact the newspapers and radio stations. She will ask Miss Skinnybones to include a notice of our lecture when Miss Skinnybones talks about events to take place. Mrs. McAstor will make all the arrangements with the hotel and she will be assisted by Mrs. Chirpbird.

There is one more matter that must be taken care of and that is the matter of naming the talk or, as it is sometimes called, "Giving it a title."

In picking a title for any subject to be discussed, we must always remember that the title will attract or repel immediately those whom we wish to bring to our meeting. If a lecture were to be given by a physicist on the subject of fissionable material and the public notices read "Fissionable Materials, Their Relationship to Modern Concepts of Atomic Energy," this title would undoubtedly frighten away many who otherwise might be interested. It sounds too highbrow —too stuffy. On the other hand, if the same lecture were to be designated "Will the Atom Blow the Earth and All Its People to Smithereens," the likelihood is that the second title would attract many more people. The reasons for this conclusion are obvious. The first sounds like a stuffed-shirt, professorial dissertation to be given by some absent-minded physicist who probably lives in an ivory tower. We expect to be handed a large number of complicated mathematical formulae that are completely over our heads. We are frightened by the possibilities that we won't even understand the first thing the lecturer is going to talk about. To ourselves we express the wish that we could understand what is going to be said at that lecture, but we're certainly not going to go, much as we would love to, because we want to know more about atoms. Now, let us look over the second title. This is a little more like it. We have an idea of what this is going to be about. Certainly we are interested in the atomic age and what it holds in store for us. We won't be around to worry if we are blown to smithereens, but we would like to get a little bit of advance notice just to see if there is a slim chance of getting out of the way before things begin to pop. Here's a talk that will be stimulating. This man talks our language. We know what the words "blown to smithereens" means. These words give us a very vivid and exciting picture of what may happen. It even gives us a thrill to think of all the important and maybe even secret things that this lecture will tell us about. An impatience to be at the lecture should be created within us. We should have the feeling that no other appointment will be made that can possibly interfere with this particular lecture. That's the reaction that a title should bring forth when anyone reads it.

Words are the instruments we use in making our ideas known to others. Words are the instruments we use in trying to impress others. People who know how to handle words can say the same thing in a number of different ways and, in each case, succeed in impressing the people they want to reach. There are some gifted individuals who can talk with the members of scientific societies, talk with children, talk with plain average citizens, and even talk to dull-witted people, and in all cases make themselves understood. When, therefore, we draft any written material concerning the announcement of a coming lecture, the words we use should be such words as attract attention and make an impression upon all the readers. All this applies to *all* kinds of meetings —not only to lectures.

Take a 'look at the two samples above. There is no "punch" in the first one, except possibly for a very small number of people who are physicists. None of the words attach themselves to our inner mind. The words go sliding

(33)

by and leave only the faintest impression about something relating to his "business" about atomic energy. It's all Greek to us. There are no sharp-sounding words that penetrate like barbs. Some words are like sharp instruments. They find their way into our inner minds and virtually nothing can get them out of there. Words that have the letters S and C, Z and K are words that make impressions upon us. The word "zero" is a good example. The word "schism" is another good example. By this time you get the point.

Even at the risk of repetition the following should be stressed: Remember always to follow the rule—whenever using written notices of any meeting or lecture, be sure to use the simplest and most impressive kind of words. Be sure to use the words that have a tendency to penetrate into the inner mind. Put your phrases together so that the words, when added up, will have power behind them, power to become part of the things that people remember, power to impress an individual who has little time to give to careful analysis.

Write out samples of phrases on separate sheets of paper. Try combining. If you reach the point where none of the examples satisfy you, then *give* up momentarily. Once you are bogged down it is best to make a new start after you have cleared your mind of the phrase-manufacturing idea.

Samples of phrases should be drafted by one or two committee members and, if possible, different individuals should be asked to choose which phrase or which group of phrases they prefer. If you are going to test the phrases, use people in different walks of life. In that way you can obtain for yourself a cross-section of opinion. This is the surest way of discovering what Mr. John Citizen thinks when he sees what you have written. The unknown individual may sometimes come up with a brand-new idea or a suggestion that

(34)

will enable you to solve completely a perplexing problem; and in addition to all this remember that one's ego is flattered when called upon to render an opinion. The flattered one is more likely to be ensnared by your wiles than the un-flattered one. It is an opening wedge into the invitation field to come to your meeting.

Just one more thing and our committee is ready to adjourn for the day. We must talk about the leaflet or the letter that is going to be mailed or distributed. There are general rules that apply to all leaflets and specific rules that apply to a very limited number. We will discuss only the general rules.

Announcements of a lecture should be on white paper. If the organization can afford the price, the paper should be of a good quality, but not too fancy nor of too high a quality. If you have any doubt in your mind about the quality of paper being used and its effectiveness, discard it. Cheap or low-quality paper has a bad effect. Always lean toward the better grade.

The plan of the leaflet or letter should highlight the *subject matter,* the *date* of the meeting, the *place,* and the *name of the lecturer.* It is not too important to have the name of the sponsoring organization conspicuously plastered all over the leaflet. A good rule to follow is to have the top of the leaflet start out with good-sized lettering. Whenever possible, use adjectives or adverbs.

Again referring back to the subject of the atom and our being blown to smithereens, a good leaflet would start out with the word *atoms,* in bold type across the top of the leaflet. Immediately thereunder, the following:

ATOMS

DATE: OCTOBER 1950 8 p. M. Sharp

PLACE: CENTRAL HOTEL
X Street   &   F Avenue

A different kind of lecture on the *Atom* by PROFESSOR CYCLOTRON, the famous inventor, physicist, author, and traveler, WHO UNTIL RECENTLY WAS THE ONLY MAN TO KNOW THE SECRET OF THE ATOMIC BOMB.

REMEMBER

CENTRAL HOTEL   October 1950

Seating capacity of the auditorium limited to—seats.
Under auspices of} }
Admission $.50

The leaflet set forth above does not pretend for a moment to *give* an exact idea of how it must be made up. It sets forth the things that should be stressed. Any new twist or angle you may think of always brings rewards. Never hesitate to do something in a different manner from what was done before. If the leaflet can be changed or improved in any way by inserting or taking out anything, by all means do so. Always be sure to *give a* great deal of attention to the *form* of your leaflet or letter, the choice of words, the type of print, the length of the leaflet, and the number of words used. The fewer words, the better—[1]if they are the right words, carefully chosen. Try hard to avoid the corny stuff. Too many people like to use the same adjectives all the time. They don't seem to have any vocabulary except "exciting, magnificent, thrilling, and charming." Take the trouble to look into the dictionary and find some synonyms

(36)

or antonyms. A few minutes spent in this kind of work may mean the difference between a successful meeting or a failure. Check the grammar in the letter or leaflet. Do not make any grammatical or spelling errors. Always check he spelling of proper nouns. There can be no excuse for the failure to spell correctly the name of any person or place. Sometimes a misspelled name can lead to a great deal of embarrassment. Avoid such a situation by being careful.

An interesting and humorous situation occurred in a rather large-sized western city several years ago. A group of businessmen had been organized for many years and from time to time they met to discuss their common problems. At each meeting a speaker was invited. The Federal Government had always been considered a reservoir that could be called upon to supply a speaker whenever the organization required one. A special problem arose and a meeting was arranged for a given day at one of the more popular hotels. Businessmen being much wiser in the art of arranging meetings than most others., they decided to combine business with some pleasure. The program of entertainment was built around the "smoker" concept. Everyone was primed for a gala event. Arrangements had been made for the government speaker to appear at a given time in the lobby of the hotel. A committee had been designated for the purpose of greeting the speaker and escorting him to the meeting room. At the appointed hour the head of the committee asked the captain of the bell boys to page Francis}. After one or two calls a rather attractive middle-aged lady approached the bell boy and said, "I am Francis}." The bell-boy captain pointed to the three gentlemen standing nearby and said politely, "These gentlemen would like to speak with you." Little did he know how great a tragedy he had just taken part in. The committee members had come prepared to meet a gentleman speaker. The report made by the committee of arrangements was to the effect that Mr. Francis   was to be the speaker. The three committee members were petrified. There had never been a female speaker addressing their organization before. The evening's entertainment was a little different from that which a lady would be expected to sit through. The committee chairman began to stutter and try to find ways of explaining his predicament. The first words out of his mouth were, "How do you do, Mrs. ———— . There must be some mistake. We were told that a Mr. Francis ———— would be the speaker." The lady was very gracious and replied, "I am sorry that this unfortunate mistake has occurred, but I am Frances. I am the Chief Statistician of the Department and I was told that your representative was advised that I was to be the designated speaker." A hurried conference was held and it was discovered that the person who had made the arrangements took it for granted that Francis ———— must be a man since only men had ever been known to be invited as speakers before this particular group. Fortunately, the entire situation was happily cleared up. The lady proved to be as effective as any male speaker had been heretofore. She delighted the entire audience and was sent on her way with paeans of praise ringing in her ears. The chairman of the arrangements committee, however, found it difficult to live down the amount of joshing to which he was subjected for a long, long time. All situations of this kind do not end happily. Therefore, you are again admonished to check carefully on the speaker where the name is definitely not that of a male or female.

Just one more point and we are through for the evening. The story is told an English Lord who came to America and tried to convince some of his friends that Americans are the most skeptical people in the world. To prove his point, the Englishman said: "I will wager that in 12 hours' time, I will not be able to sell 10 five-dollar gold pieces at a quarter per piece." (Yes, there used to be five-dollar gold pieces in our country.) The Englishman posted himself at the middle of the Brooklyn Bridge and stood there offering five-dollar gold pieces at $.25 per piece. Suffice it to say—he won the wager. The moral of this story is "*Don't try to give away anything for nothing to an American audience. Always charge those who come to look or listen. Americans love to pay for anything and everything.*" Our museums are fine examples of treasures standing like tombstones in an unpeopled world. The numbers that visit the museums are pathetically small. Very recently in the city of New York, one of the museums had an exhibit of the works of a famous artist. The museum decided to charge an entrance fee. This is not the usual custom followed by a museum. Tens of thousands of persons went to see the exhibit; yet it is a matter of record that upon hundreds of occasions, when the museum had other notable exhibits, the number of persons who came to view the art on display was modest in comparison to the throngs who crowded their way into the hall when an admission fee was imposed. Bear this in mind always.

If you are going to have a lecture, charge and you'll get an audience. Don't be afraid to charge a dollar and even more. Only be certain that you choose the right time, place, subject matter, 'lecturer, and that you exploit every avenue of advertising. Income from lectures can be used for better and still better work.

The committee now stands adjourned until we meet again to discuss further work in the field of meetings and to take up a number of other problems in that connection.

(39)

Chapter 2

HOW TO GET YOUR MAN

IT IS VERY surprising to find that in many organizations, the person or persons in charge of planning lectures or forums or other events of a similar nature do not have the faintest idea of where to go or where to look in order to find speakers for a given occasion. To those who do know it is very simple, so why not let yourself into the society of the "cognoscenti" ?

We shall take a situation in which a speaker is wanted for . a talk on "Rare Plants in the Tibet country." (Rare subject too.) At first blush it would seem difficult, but it really is not so. The principal subject is related to plants. Plants mean botany. This is the science concerned with plant life. The proper place to look *is* in any source book that lists botanists or botanical societies. There are source books in ⁱ libraries, in museums, and in schools. Suppose then, for some unexplainable reason, no source book can be found. What then ? Try another tack. Get hold of a copy of *Who's Who* and check through the lists. The likelihood of success is almost 100 percent. Men and women of every walk of life are listed in *Who's Who*.

It is in libraries and schools that the greatest number of source books may be found. In every library some department or section is set aside for source purposes only. Not only are the books available but cross indexes are frequently found.

(40)

If the person seeking information is not familiar with the method of using an index, the librarian can invariably be depended on to help. It may be said that as a general rule librarians as a group are the persons most willing to help anyone who requests it. They seem to be able to get the answer to almost any problem for any citizen. When all else fails, the library and librarian can be depended on to come through. Too few people realize the work of librarians. They are taken for granted and are generally considered thoroughly trained human indexes for lazy readers to ask questions of. By and large the librarian is a well-trained person who is capable of cutting short the average man's search for certain kinds of information. The librarian's business is to know how to use books as tools and as pleasure-giving objects. They know their stock in trade and are always happy to take part in a search for something they have but cannot describe in detail at the moment. Thus, in a search for an authority on a given subject it is helpful to put the problem before your librarian. Cultivate the librarian's friendship and he or she will work with you in your search as though it were a game. In larger libraries such as the 42nd Street Library in New York City, there is virtually nothing one can ask for that some librarian will not be able to help you find. When we say cultivate your librarian's friendship we do not mean to throw the burden upon the librarian. What we do mean is that the librarian will help those who are willing to help themselves.

It is amazing to find so many schools just waiting for the opportunity to serve, with no one coming to them with requests. Within the last few years our country has been swept by the adult education movement. Each day the program expands. There are thousands of men and women working in this program who can qualify as speakers before your organization. Seek out the local school where adult education courses are given and you will be certain to get results.

In addition to adult education there is the well-known extension course system. These extension courses are usually part of the work of colleges and universities and closely resemble adult education work. Again the likelihood of success in your quest for a speaker is great. It is true that some colleges or universities are more frequently called on to send speakers or help in educational work than some others are, but it is also true that those connected with colleges are all too frequently classed as long-haired or pedantic or stuffy. This idea is nonsensical and should be eradicated.

Once upon a time the college professor had to assume the cloistered air. It was expected of him. Laymen thought it was like living in a different world to be an inmate of "a school of higher learning." All this is ended. The secret is out. Everyone now knows that professors eat and sleep and work and worry like everyone else. We all know that they work hard for little pay, are frequently influenced by the power of the tycoons' pay check, and that they frequently have to fear for their jobs. The alumni boss the trustees, the trustees boss the college president, the college president bosses the professors, and the professors boss the unfortunates who hope to become professors. So you see, the teachers in colleges and universities are humans and many of them would be happy to avail themselves of the opportunity to speak to others besides students. In situations where inexperienced persons must tackle the work of the education committee it is suggested that the nearest college be contacted and the department involved in the subject be asked to help out. Where a member of an education committee goes to a college department head to seek help, he or she should do so with the idea in mind of laying the entire problem before

(42)

the professor. Ask as many questions as you can get answers to. The answers to questions make up the difference between the neophyte and the experienced member.

Remember too that radio stations as a rule have information about qualified speakers. Their sustaining programs are valuable and consist in part of groups of men and women working in given fields of endeavor. One of these fields of endeavor may cover the very topic to be discussed at your meeting. Call the station and try the public relations department.

It is a fact that some of the suggestions above cannot sometimes be taken for one reason or another. The use of one's imagination is important. Just because the work is limited to a very small field doesn't mean that the searcher cannot use his or her imagination. The answers to problems can be gotten from the most unexpected sources. Go to another source. Pick up a telephone book and check for the type of organization most likely to give you a lead to the speaker being sought. Going back to our subject above, we begin by looking under "Botanic." There are Botanic Societies, Botanic Gardens, Botanic Exhibits, etc. Take one or all and begin making inquiries. If you don't ask you won't get—so you do ask the person at the Botanic Society. "Does your organization have a speaker's or lecture bureau?" If the party at the other end says "Yes," you follow through with another question, "Do you have anyone who is an authority on plants in Tibet?" "No." "Can you tell me where I can find a speaker who is conversant with plant life in Tibet?" The person on the other end thinks for a moment and suggests, "Why not try the botanist in charge of tropical plants? He knows of the different kinds of specialists.. ." And so you keep trying. The more you get bounced from one prospect to the other, the more you learn. In the end you will get

(43)

your man (or woman, who knows?). Make notes of everything you are told. The information may not be just what you need at the moment but it can be helpful on some other occasion. Building up the information bureau of your society is a very important job and an accumulation of data gathered in the course of searching may save much time and effort later.

Did you ever think of the possibility of writing to the local newspaper or a popular magazine for assistance in locating just the type of speaker you yearn for? No? Try it and you will be happily surprised. Newspapers and magazines have "morgues" full of all sorts of useless and even useful information. Nothing is lost by trying.

Almost every newspaper and hundreds of magazines have departments devoted to gardening and other matters botanical. All newspapers and magazines of any importance are divided into departments. Each department is headed by a special editor and these editors in turn are men and women who are recognized and qualified authorities in their fields. It is a safe statement to say that the likelihood of their being able to help is almost 99 percent certain. The editor of each department is very anxious to reach as much of the public as is possible. Contact with the public builds circulation and large circulation means jobs. Every letter received by one of these editors adds another rock of security to his job. When you write, the paper or magazine is thus informed that another citizen looks upon *it* as part of his *modus vivendi.* (The uninitiated who do not know what *modus vivendi* means should take the trouble this very moment to look up the phrase up in their old Latin ponies or in a big Webster dictionary.)

The example under discussion is typical of any other problem of a similar nature. Of course, in some fields it's a

(44)

snap to find what's wanted in the line of speakers; but in other fields the job is a difficult one. Take politics—that ought to be easy, but it's not. There are scores, yes, hundreds of political clubs and other types of organizations interested in political matters, but that does not mean that an intelligent and tolerable speaker on political subjects is easy to find. In this case it is wise to start at the top.

If our meeting is taken up with a problem of great national or international importance, and the meeting is planned on a very grand scale, the search for a speaker is directed at the top levels. This speaker must have stature, reputation, real knowledge, etc. This is not just another of many events. It is particularly important that it be on a high level. Always bear in mind that no one is too important or too big to be approached. Anyone is approachable if the proper technique is used. The best technique is the direct straightforward approach.

In political life there is always some sort of national organization to which one can write and ask all kinds of questions or make any kind of request. In all probability the national office will pass the request on to a lower office and at the same time will supply the inquirer with sufficient leads to open the field wide. In a short time the search will be narrowed to the confines of the speakers' bureau of the state or city political organization. You will receive communications from one of the local secretaries, supplying names and addresses and brief biographies of prospects. A bit of thought plus the will to seek is all that is necessary to put one on the road to discovery.

In meetings that are purely local there is always the danger that incompetent speakers will be supplied. This is truer of politics than of anything else. In political meetings of a local nature the average speaker is a superficial individual

(45)

who utters the usual formulas and shibboleths that amount to nothing. Some politicians are political scientists as well as politicians. These individuals are rare in the major political parties, but they can be found. The minority political parties, on the other hand, specialize in this sort of rare bird.

The reference made to editors of matters botanical in newspapers and magazines applies with equal, if not greater, force to editors of matters political, financial, cultural, etc. No doubt the chances are that there are more editors in matters political, financial, cultural, etc. than in some other fields. Check up and convince yourself. In the process of checking you are learning something you did not know before.

Besides all that has been written above, there are still two simple ways of discovering and getting speakers. One: Ask some of the members of the organization if they can give names of qualified persons or leads to qualified speakers. You have a surprise in store.

Some organizations have many members on their rolls. These members do not always make known all the facts about their connections. Frequently a member belongs to other societies or clubs, and one of these may be just the place to go for the speaker we want. Besides belonging to other groups, members may have hobbies that involve contact with men and women who are expert in little-known subjects or broad fields. The way to find out is to ask or by sending out questionnaires. The use of questionnaires may give much information that would otherwise never be known. Each member should be asked to fill one out.

Two: Ask friends or relatives to help. The fact that the fellow you are asking is your brother or your ever-bragging brother-in-law does not mean that he cannot *give* you a good name or a good suggestion.

Speakers are as anxious to be found out as you are to find them. Seek and you shall discover.

One of the most common places to look for a speaker we have not discussed at all—that is, the professional lecture bureau. Up to this point our thoughts have been about the organizations which have no budget for paid speakers. We shall now assume that the organization does have money to pay. In that case a. reputable lecture bureau is the place to go. Such bureaus will look about for a speaker if they do not have one available. That is how they make their money.

Whenever possible, speakers should be paid. If the speaker does not want to accept money, the group that sends him should be offered the money. If they don't want the money a gift should be given to the speaker. Some sort of a token must be offered to show appreciation. Expenses should always be paid as well as food and shelter provided.

An interesting story is told about a famous authoress who delivered a very fine talk to a women's group. At the end of the talk the president, with a grand flourish, proceeded to tender to the speaker a check for her lecture. It seems that the authoress felt the group was doing good work and she wished to use her fee as a contribution to the cause. She turned to the president and offered the check back to her, whereupon the president insisted that the contribution could not be accepted without the consent of the committee. The speaker agreed to wait while the president convened the committee in special session in an anteroom. In a little while the president returned and told the speaker that the committee had voted to accept the check. She climaxed her profusion of words with this statement to the speaker: "And we intend to use this money as part of a fund to get the best speakers for our members." Of course we all know what she meant, but she put it pretty badly. Money can do strange things and create even stranger situations.

One final word about getting speakers. Somewhere in the past the records may show talks on the same or similar subjects and may also contain names of speakers who were well received on other occasions. Many speakers have proven acceptable to organizations on more than one occasion. The fact that it is the same speaker does not mean he must speak on the same subject or *give* the same talk.

In addition to the notes of previous meetings there may be newspaper clippings relating to the particular subjects. Where an organization is devoted to one special type of endeavor, it is easy and wise to have a research bureau in which clippings are accumulated. This sort of clipping bureau is invaluable not only for the speakers' bureau but for a number of other purposes.

Chapter 3

AT LAST-THE MEETING

NIGHTS AND DAYS we have spent worrying and hoping and sometimes dying a thousand deaths, while we waited for that meeting to come off. If only the dang-busted thing were over with. What a relief that will be. Take it easy! It will all come out fine. Someday it will make a good story to recall and retell.

Think back on some of the anxious moments you have had in the past. At the time of the event or before it happened, it seemed as though all the bad luck in the world were yours. Things seem to come so easy to others but not to you. Well, it isn't so at all, is it? There are others who have enjoyed good fortune and misfortune just as you have— and now you tell the story over and over again. Yes, you tell the story over and over again even when the ending was not so happy. It makes a good anecdote. It is part of the interesting conversation with the friends at the dinner table or the stranger on the plane or that interesting old lady sitting all alone in a drawing room on the Pullman. Cheer up. . . .

Here we are, folks. Tonight the meeting of our society takes place. Yes, the committee did get notices in the newspapers. The local radio gossipmongers mentioned the meeting. The children of a number of members as well as some of the members themselves did a swell job distributing cards and leaflets, and many of the members called their friends and relatives. The meeting simply must be a success. Now it is all in your lap, friend reader, because you are going to be the chairman of the evening. What to do! What to do! Follow these rules and you will do just fine.

First: Go to the place of meeting between one-half to three-quarters of an hour ahead of time. When you get there early you can check on all of the details.

Second: Begin checking all the details that must be attended to. (a) Is all the literature on hand that is to be distributed to the audience?(b) Is there a flag available? (c) Be sure to have the banner of the society conspicuously displayed. If you do not have a banner, you should have a neat sign with large, plain, clear lettering giving the full name of your organization, its address, and the name of the secretary, (d) Have a table or lectern available for the speaker to put his notes on—or to lean on if he feels that he needs it. See to it that the table or lectern is equipped either with a good light or is located in a well-lighted spot, (e) Have paper cups and a pitcher of fresh clean water. If you use a glass pitcher make sure the grease spots have been removed. The same is true about drinking glasses. Be sure the glasses sparkle. It adds to the charm of the meeting.

This may seem like a trifling detail—and it is. But it's just such a trifle that can mar a well-planned meeting. Take this situation, for example. In one of the largest cities in the United States, a convention of health officers was being held. At the time in question a prominent epidemiologist was holding forth. He was telling the ways in which epidemics may spread. He referred to insect-contaminated foods, human carriers, etc., and then stopped as he leaned over to pick up a glass of water to quench his thirst. As he did so, he held up the glass to the audience and smilingly said to the assemblage, "Yes, and maybe even through persistent smudges of lipstick." He replaced the glass of water and did not make another attempt to quench his thirst even though one of the committee members hastened to place a clean glass with fresh water near at hand. This embarrassing situation was never lived down. The damage had been done. It all could have been avoided if only the committee member in charge had taken the time to do his duty.

(f) If a number of persons are to occupy the platform, see to it that there are enough chairs available—that is, chairs that are in good condition. Place them in such position as will *give* each person ample room and at the same time will not block a full view of the speaker and the audience. Always provide one chair for yourself as chairman. You never appear as ridiculous to the audience as when you go hunting for a seat after introducing the speaker, (g) Provide scratch paper and several pencils with sharpened points, (h) Check with each committee member and see to it that each member has attended to every detail assigned to him. If not, take the matter up with the proper authority.

By the time you have checked everything outlined above it is 7:45. The audience has begun to arrive. What do you do now? Take out those notes you made (or should have made) about the name and position in life of the speaker or speakers. Fill in any details that may be missing. Read your notes over very slowly and carefully. This checking of notes takes only a minute or two. Got nothing to worry about? You are lucky. Nothing gone wrong? You must be sleeping and dreaming. Let it go at that. Here comes one of those people who is going to sit on the platform. He may look like a fat-headed moron to you, but you must greet him warmly. Get up from that chair with precision and snap. Advance as though you really mean to welcome the fellow. Introduce yourself. Give your name in a clear audible manner. Repeat the name of the guest if you know it. Ask his name if you don't. Be sure you get that name. Write it down. Take your time. Pronounce it correctly. Have a committee member offer to take charge of his hat and coat or any other things he may be carting along. Don't yank his briefcase from him if he insists upon keeping it. Let him keep it! If the guest is a lady, don't ask for her hat and coat. Offer to assist her with her wraps. Women love that bearskin called a "wrap," so you or your committee member ask for the lady's wrap. Don't grab her bag—that's half her life. There's frequently more in her bag than you can possibly imagine. Very timidly ask if she would like to have her bag put away with her wraps. If the lady gives up her bag, guard it with the life of a committee member. Imagine what would happen if she lost her bag! You do the imagining—we are afraid to.

Please note carefully. Wherever and whenever possible, meet and greet all speakers and special guests in an anteroom or somewhere that keeps you and them out of view of the audience. Introduce those guests and speakers who do not know one another. Repeat each one's name in a clear, firm manner. Get the conversation going.

The time is now 7:55. The meeting is to start at 8 P. M. This is the moment when you take over in full. You tell the speaker or speakers what the procedure at the meeting is to be like; how much time the speaker may take. Where there is a single speaker the rule generally is that the chairman and the speaker arrange the time schedule. If the speaker is to be permitted as much time as he sees fit to take, then no arrangement is to be made for signals. The speaker does his own timing. If the arrangement is for a limited time, then the chairman should arrange to *give* the speaker a signal—5 minutes—before the expiration of the time set, a second signal—2 minutes— before the expiration of time, and finally a signal that time is up. If for any reason the speaker fails or refuses to heed the final time signal, the chairman should put a note in front of the speaker and remind him that the time has run out. The chairman should take over without allowing too much drag of time. All of the above applies of course to single speakers. Where there are two or more speakers, the time is held strictly to the minute—and no dillydallying. Signals should be definite and the chairman should see to it that each speaker has become cognizant of the signals. If there are a number of speakers, tell each one *exactly* how much time each may take. If you are going to give warning signals at the 5-minute mark, the 2-minute mark, and the finish, tell the speaker or speakers exactly how you are going to do it. *Let the speakers know you mean business when you say that they must stop at the end of their allotted time.* Smile when you tell it to them but be sure to get it across with no if s, ands, or buts.

When you have finished telling the speaker or speakers about the time arrangements, you tell the guests where they are to be seated. It is 7:59 P.M. Stand at the door leading to the platform or dais and invite the speaker and guests to go out and take their seats. Guests go first. Give them each a nod as they pass you. At last it is your turn. You go straight out to the table or lectern and prepare to open the meeting. It is 8 P.M. *Right now* you start. Not before—not later. Right on time. Never keep the audience waiting. That's impressive. You are standing there straight and looking out at the audience. Count to yourself. One. Two. Three. Wait for absolute silence! If the audience doesn't quiet down in a moment or two, tap very lightly. Wait again. If they are subsiding, keep waiting. Let them know by your actions and attitude that you are running the show. Be big and powerful in their eyes. When the chairman encounters any difficulty in obtaining quiet, he must use every trick there is to get the audi-ience to come to attention. This is done in a number of ways, but the most effective is to begin speaking in a low voice with the stare of the chairman fixed on those in the first few aisles in front of him. As soon as those in the rear see the chairman talking to the ones up front the "rear guard" will begin to clamor for silence. They want to know what's going on. Their curiosity is aroused and curiosity is a strong force for self-discipline. Under no circumstances whatsoever is the chairman to shout.

On rare occasions there may be some justification for opening the meeting late. When the weather is very bad or if there has been some very exciting event in the locality and the people haven't settled down to their normal way of life— you may hold up the meeting for 10 to 15 minutes.

You begin to speak. The big question is: do you know what to say? You appear not to be sure. Then let us tell you—but first we are going to look you over and see how impressive you are.

HOW YOU LOOK TO THE AUDIENCE

When you are chairman, it is very important that you pay particular attention to the way you look. You don't have to look like a Venus or an Adonis. The looks of a Cary Grant or Dorothy Lamour will do. It's chiefly your dress we're concerned with at the moment.

As chairman you should dress in a dignified, well-groomed, unostentatious manner—in a word, plainly and in good taste. What difference does your manner of dress make? A lot of difference, we say. Take, for example, a chairman who is dressed in a very sharp form-fitting suit, one that is common-

iy called "flashy," and now add to it the picture of the same chairman wearing a bright yellow tie made in a large Windsor knot and on that yellow tie are brilliant red spots with jet-black arrows piercing each red spot. Do you have that picture in mind? You do? Fine. Now add to that a pair of loud tan pointed shoes and a light pink shirt tight around the neck, so tight that the chairman looks as though he is going to choke to death. Can you see that chairman up there in front ? He looks like a proud, strutting peacock who accidentally got out of the cage. This of course is exaggerated but we are purposely exaggerating in order to drive home the idea. No one would dare appear in such a get-up as is here described, but a close resemblance has been known to exist between the chairman pictured above and some seen on the platform in the flesh. A good chairman always gives thought to the way he or she dresses for the meeting. "How *should* a perfect chairman be dressed?" you may ask. That's a good question and very simply answered. Here goes for the male. Rule 1: Wear a plain suit—not too light nor a gloomy-looking black one. A blue suit is always in good taste. Rule 2: The tie must be a quiet one. Not a dead color. A pleasant-looking quiet one. Rule 3: Be sure to have your shoes shined. A chairman all dressed up with unshined shoes is like a man with a three-day growth of beard dressed in a tuxedo. Rule 4: Keep your socks in place with garters or at least have socks with garter tops. The sloppy look is O.K. for the collegiate type but not for a good chairman. Rule 5: Your hair must be neatly combed (not slicked down and shining like a headlight in the dark) and you must be clean-shaven. Rule 6: Have your hands clean and your nails free of the earth's crust. Rule 7: Never wear flashing diamonds or a wrist watch that sparkles like a Tiffany jewel exhibit. Rule 8: Wear a plain white shirt with a comfortable collar.

(55)

Rule 9: Have a white handkerchief neatly folded in your front upper jacket pocket. No flower in the lapel. No diverting ribbons or buttons. Now you look swell.

Suppose you're a female. Very well. First of all you cannot be a chairman—you will be a chairlady. There is a difference. We can prove it—but it all adds up to the same thing. Even a chairlady should not look like a dressed-up circus horse. There is something special about chairladies. Frequently they specialize in looking like overdressed fashion shows or they appear to be models of the cellar clothes line with the cleaned floor rags hanging from it.

A chairlady who is dressed in a well-fitting suit with an attractive blouse is a picture that is lovely to behold. A solid-colored dress with appropriate simple jewelry can be worn instead of a suit. A chairlady may, without causing any comment or audience distraction, wear a flower. A flower that will not compel the small minds in the audience to spend their time wondering where the chairlady got it. A rose or maybe two in the form of a small corsage is permissible. Two is tasteful—more than two makes the chairlady appear like the winning horse with the flower horseshoe around its neck. Never wear an orchid. Such a luxury is not found in sand lots. It costs money and raises many an eyebrow unnecessarily. It knocks the whole idea of a well-poised, confident, and capable chairlady into a cocked hat—and speaking of hats brings us to the question of a chairlady's wearing a hat. It's all right for a chairlady to wear a hat provided it is not too gay and provided further it is smaller than a beach umbrella. A chic little hat without birds fluttering around the crown or a display of citrus fruit can and does add to the attractiveness of a chairlady. If it's your hat we're talking about and it has a feather in it or on it, be sure the feather is small and doesn't flutter around like a weather vane.

By this time you pretty much have the idea of how a chairman or chairlady should dress. Let's go back to the meeting we were about to open at 8 P.M. sharp.

You are standing at the table looking out at the audience. They are quiet and you are about to speak. Take it easy. First you welcome the audience, the special guests, and the speakers. You do it in somewhat the following manner: "Ladies and Gentlemen, honored guests and friends of the Society for the Preservation of Moth Balls: as Chairman of the evening, I want to welcome all of you on behalf of the Society and to tell you that it is a pleasure to have you here." You have done a complete job in one short sentence. You have warmly expressed a pleasant feeling to the guests and the assembly. People do enjoy kind words and will always respond by giving their attention to the business at hand. Proceed. You take care of the next step which is that of referring to the arrangements committee. Take a moment or two to mention them and their work. If the committee is a small one, mention all the names. Only on the rarest of occasions should you single out any one member for particular praise. Do so only if the other committee members are enthusiastic about the accomplishment of the one outstanding member. If there is the slightest chance of causing friction, you forget it. Your thanks to the committee is in simple terms with no question about your sincerity. Use something like this: "This wonderful meeting is the result of the combined efforts of the Society's committee on education of which Mr. X is the proud chairman. I do hope that in the course of the evening, the opportunity will present itself for the chairman to tell a bit about the tremendous amount of time and effort that was spent. The presence of so large a gathering is a demonstration of the success the committee has achieved. For this success, the Chair expresses the thanks

(57)

of our Society for a tough job wonderfully executed." To repeat, only if the committee is small, mention their names: Mr. 1, Mr. 2, Mrs. 3, Miss 4, and Mr. X, chairman.

What does the chairman do if the meeting is poorly attended despite the efforts of the committee? He goes right ahead thanking the committee and in fact is more intent on showing them the appreciation of the organization. He says, "Sometimes a man and his colleagues labor long and hard but their fellow men fail to appreciate what is being done for them. Our committee on education has done a wonderful job but not enough people know what the committee did to make this fine evening possible. The subject was carefully chosen. It is fine and, of course, interesting. To be sure that the subject is adequately and expertly presented, the committee secured the services of Professor ——————— as the speaker for this evening. If they did nothing else they would be entitled to our sincere thanks. To Mr. 1, Mr. *2,* Mrs. 3, Miss 4, and Mr. X, chairman of the committee, we say: You have done a real good job. Those of us who are here are the gainers, the absentees are the losers. Thank you very much for your efforts." In this way you encourage the active members. They deserve to be encouraged and the chairman owes it to them to say so.

Move along now. You have about four or five minutes at your disposal. Next step. The purpose of the meeting. As you well know, there are a thousand different reasons why meetings are held or called. The principles governing the presentation of an opening statement are always the same. You state the subject in broad terms. For example: "This meeting has been called by the XYZ Society to protest the vivisection of paramecia." There you have it. You have told the audience that the meeting was called by a particular society and also you have stated the purpose of the meeting. Now you come to that part of your work as chairman that requires real skill. For a minute or so you are going to "warm up" the subject—that is, you will tell about the widespread interest in the sufferings of the millions of paramecia. Refer to the many newspaper editorials and the court actions that have been commenced to stop this sort of practice. The subject is a very important one and the Society is adding its voice of protest to the many other heard round the world. You know the kind of tripe most chairmen hand out. World importance. Burning issue. Voice of protest, etc. etc. Enough. Don't talk too much. Remember we have a speaker. Get going and bring on the speaker. Start the introduction. "Some years ago an outstanding scholar decided to give the subject the attention it deserved. As a result of his years of research, he has written among other fascinating books, *The Subconscious Reactions of Paramecia to External Cutting Stimuli,* a Literary Chill-of-the-Month selection. His *Encyclopedia of the Flea Kingdom* is soon to be issued by Hard Press, Inc. It is an honor to introduce the eminent humanitarian and champion of flea control, Professor Exilias Minibrain of Pinewood." Applause. Turn half way around. Face the rising speaker. Nod ever so slightly and wait until he begins that first tottering step toward the speakers' table. Permit him to pass in front of you, then you slink out of the way to the chair which you made sure was in place for you. The speaker has reached the table and has already begun to make sounds. Does that mean that you can doze off or start puffing on your odoriferous pipe? It does not. You are the human funnel through which every happening of the evening flows. Your poise, your charm, your ability to project your personality are still felt by the audience. Sit there and look interested even if it kills you. Keep your eye chiefly on the speaker. (That's what you *get*

(59)

for being chairman. Next time you'll know better.) Occasionally, you slowly and not too conspicuously look about at the audience but in a moment or two you come back to the speaker. Mr. Chairman: you must keep your eyes and ears open.

Here are a few do's and don'ts:

1. Don't engage anyone next to you in conversation.

2. Don't start smoking because there is nothing more interesting to do.

3. Don't permit any committee or society members to move about on the platform. No tiptoeing around in back of you.

4. Don't chew gum or candy or your fingernails.

5. Don't keep looking at your watch.

6. Don't blow your nose so that it sounds like a thunderclap.

Here are some do's:

1. Keep an interested look on your face.

2. Try to sense the reaction of the audience to the speaker.

3. Be prepared for any emergency by watching everything that is going on.

4. Think of the way in which you are going to introduce the next speaker if there is to be one.

5. Check with yourself the arrangement for the question or discussion period if there is to be one.

Some thirty minutes have gone by and the speaker has just concluded. The audience applauds the speaker and you prepare to rise. Don't jump up to take over again. Wait. Count to yourself. Listen to the volume of applause. If it's just that polite kind that gives you a sick feeling in the pit of your abdomen, be prepared to step in by the time you have counted three. If the applause is full and hearty and the

(60)

speaker has made a hit with the crowd, wait. Instead of counting three, count six or seven or eight. Let the applause sink in like rain o>n a summer's day. It feels good and refreshing. The speaker likes it. The audience talks by applause. Make yourself inconspicuous until that very exact moment when the enthusiasm is about to start going downhill. That's the time to step in. Place yourself again squarely in front of the audience, but be sure that you have nodded first to the speaker in a one-eighth bow and that he has located his seat. Even though you can't be heard, say "Thank you" to the retreating speaker. You will repeat it again in a moment. The audience is quiet. You speak. "Thank you, Professor Minibrain. That was a thrilling talk" [if you mean it]; or: "Thank you, Professor Minibrain—and now we come to the next part of the program which is our question period." You may proceed with the question period without any waiting. Tell the people how they are to put their questions. If the questions are to be written, have committee members on the floor with paper and pencils. Take time out to give the members a chance to distribute paper and to collect the questions. While this *is* being done, keep up a running conversation with the audience (in which you do all the talking), interspersed with announcements of future events, an appeal for membership, and anything else you want to tell them about. If the questions are to be oral, you tell them how and when questions may be asked. Questions must be questions and not statements or arguments. Start from your right—go to the center and then to the left. If there is a group in the balcony you go to the right main floor and then the right balcony followed by the center main floor and the center balcony; then to the left main floor and the left balcony. Be firm about questions being short and to the point. No exceptions. You are the boss.

(61)

It's your job and no appeal may be taken. Show your strength. Here are a few rules to observe during question period.

(1) Always repeat the question *exactly* as put. Repeat it in a loud clear voice. No editorializing. Whenever a question is put to a speaker, the chairman is under obligation to repeat the question exactly as it is put by the questioner. There is a presumption that a person using language to express himself does so with the idea in mind that the words he uses are the words best suited to express what he has in mind. If he cannot do so he may ask the chairman for assistance. The chairman is only the conveyor of the question asked. He conveys the question to the speaker. The chairman does *not* have the right to do any editorializing. When the chairman takes it upon himself to editorialize he takes away the democratic right of the questioner to express himself as he sees fit.

(2) As soon as you have repeated the question, step aside without show or effort. Let the speaker do the answering. Move to the rear of the speaker and off to the side. Wait until he has finished his answer and then move forward for another question. Having gotten one, you move back as before. Keep this up until a good number of questions have been asked and answered.

(3) Insist that every person who asks a question do so in an orderly and well-mannered fashion. If the question is insulting, obstreperous or generally obnoxious, you sit the questioner down and refuse to accept his question. An audience is always disappointed when a question period is ended abruptly. They should be given warning by the chairman that the questions are to stop very shortly, say after two or three more questions. When the chairman announces that there will be only three more questions or two more ques-

(62)

tions, he must stick to that number and not relent. To do so is to be unfair to all those whose questions have been left unanswered. Sometimes a "big shot" thinks he has a special right to ask the last question after everyone else has been shut off. Nothing doing. Big shot or no big shot—what goes for one goes for all.

If there is to be a discussion period, set aside time for discussion. Don't be sloppy about it. Allot twenty minutes for questions and fifteen minutes for discussion; or make any other reasonable arrangement. Announce it to the assembly and see to it that the procedure is adhered to.

The discussion period is always a difficult time for the chairman. There is always the discussion hog. He is the first to ask for the floor. Never wants to stop talking. Is ready to take on all comers and sputters all over himself. Whenever possible the chairman should diplomatically avoid recognizing this breed of nuisance. If he must be recognized he should be held strictly to time.

Coming back to the start of the discussion period, we should bear in mind that the chairman should announce the amount of time to be allotted.

So far the evening has gone fine. You opened on time—you made all preliminary arrangements work well—you gave the arrangements committee a break and you handled the speaker well. The question and discussion period has now ended and you come to the close of the meeting. You are back in the same position where you were at 8 P.M. Be careful. Don't spoil a good evening's work. In just about two minutes it will all be over, so take it easy. Close in something like the following manner: "The time has come when we must end this meeting. It has been a very exciting and informative one. It brought out a goodly crowd and for that we are indebted to Mr. A for his work in the publicity, Mr. B for his work in

(63)

making the arrangements in this auditorium, and Mrs. C for her fine handling of literature distribution and organization of the personal telephone campaign, and to Mr. X, the chairman, for his businesslike and thorough job of coordinating all the activities of the committee. Our thanks to all of them." Applause. Continue. "Add to all of the good work of the committee, the fact that they were so fortunate to get for us so stimulating a speaker. He has given us so much to think about that we may well have to ask him to return for another session and maybe answer the scores of questions he was prevented from answering because of the shortage of time. It is a pleasure to thank Professor Minibrain again and express the hope that he will be with us again, soon. To all of you, the Society's thanks for coming. This meeting stands adjourned. Good night." Now you start the second wind-up. Immediately go over to the speaker. Pump his hand heartily and with your warmest smile and sincerity pouring out of every sweat gland, you tell the learned professor again, "Thank you for making this a wonderful meeting. Everyone was thrilled. You'll probably have a million invitations from other organizations." Step aside for a moment and let the others at him. You speak a few words to this guest and to that one. When the speaker begins to move in the direction of his sequestered hat and coat, you go along. See to it that he is set merrily on his way. Wait until most of the guests have gone and then you can go out and get yourself a full breath of fresh air and heave a sigh of relief, feel kindly toward the whole world and mutter, "Thank goodness that's over with." Now, just as a bit of dessert, read the following, reprinted by special permission from *The Nation* of May 13, 1950, by Robert Bendiner and Margaret Marshall.

(64)

BESIDE THE POINT

By now everyone who has ever suffered the agonies of prolonged after-dinner oratory knows the heroic story of Dr. Millikan. In years to come schoolboys will memorize the speech he made a few weeks ago, when, as guest of honor, he was finally called upon after three hours of preliminary build-up. "It is much too late for speechmaking," he began. "If you want to know what I would have said, read the chapter entitled 'The Road to Peace' in the forthcoming *Autobiography of Robert A. Millikan.*" Then the great man sat down.

With this inspiration I have undertaken to prepare, for use on various occasions, a timely batch of model speeches of similar honesty and conciseness. Please order by style number as shown in catalogue:

No. 112-A (for tory Republican candidates for Congress) : The government in Washington is spending too much money. If you send me to Congress I promise to vote against every appropriation except for new post offices, courthouses, and battle monuments in this Congressional District and for subsidies to you lima-bean growers who are the backbone of this community. To hell with the other districts.

No. 112-B (for liberal Democratic candidates): I ask you, my friends, only to remember that great President— Franklin Delano Roosevelt.

No. 112-C (for liberal Republican candidates): Me too.

No. 112 (for candidates in general): It is no particular pleasure for me to be here in your community, which frankly means nothing to me. I am here because politics is my bread and butter. I do not begrudge you people a living, and I trust you will not begrudge me mine. By electing me you will save yourselves, as taxpayers, that much more in unemployment insurance. Just remember that on November 7. Thank you.

No. 85 (for a chairman called on to introduce the speaker of the evening): Ladies and Gentlemen, this is Dr. Ralph Breckenfoos, who has kindly consented to come here this evening and *give* us the routine address he has been making all over the country. We are indebted to the speaker, the exact amount being $320.50, including expenses. Dr. Breckenfoos—

No. 97 (for a celebrity who has just received the annual award of the Society for the Preservation of the Whooping Crane) : This is indeed a dubious arrangement. You get a first-class drawing-card and a few thousand dollars of free publicity. I get some alleged prestige which I don't need and a pair of spun-glass book-ends. In view of the obvious imbalance, I dare say you will hardly expect a free speech into the bargain. Thank you.

No. 197-X (for a government scientist asked to address an open forum on the problems of atomic energy) : I have been authorized to tell you that the bomb which was dropped on Hiroshima in 1945 was of an atomic nature. These bombs are highly dangerous. It would be indiscreet of me to say any more about them, but if you want basic information on the subject I suggest you get hold of any current high-school physics textbook. Or better still, consult your local foreign agent.

No. 127 (for a Russian delegate to the United Nations, or fraction thereof): Mr. Chairman and my esteemed colleagues: Nyet.

R.B.

(66)

A chairman of a meeting is like the mother of triplets— every moment is full of new possibilities. You never can tell what may happen. There are some things that happen at almost every meeting, as for example:

(1) Cross-conversation while the meeting is in progress. You know the kind of ill-mannered pest who makes his way into every gathering. He always has something to say about everything at the wrong time and the wrong place. Generally speaking, intelligent people know enough to keep their mouths shut at public meetings. What then do you do when there is cross-conversation? At first you disregard it. After a moment or two it may be over. If it persists, you put on your sternest look and point your gaze directly and deliberately at the culprit or culprits. It's a safe bet that someone near the chatterbox will nudge him between the fifth and sixth rib and signal to him to stop the gabbing. Suppose you have in the audience one of those persons who doesn't give a hoot about anyone else. He is the only one who should be heard, at least so he thinks. No signal or suggestion will close him up. The people all around that noisy nuisance are annoyed by him. He deserves no mercy. Sail right into him in a quiet and very dignified manner. Soft of tone and hard of purpose—that's the idea. Walk up to the invited speaker and beg his pardon for the interruption. Stop him. Without any further ado you say, "Will the persons carrying on the meeting in the middle of the room please be courteous and kind enough to permit the speaker to continue?" This is a cruel piece of business but sometimes it must be done. Do it only when you are in full control of the meeting. It's a job that only an expert can do. It must be done with finesse. The entire incident should be over in less than ten seconds. It must never be permitted to drag on. The instant you have put the culprit in his place, you immed-

(67)

iately face the speaker, apologize again for the interruption, and proceed directly to your seat.

There is a variation of this situation you should keep in mind. Sometimes you are chairman of a meeting where everyone knows everyone else and the speaker seems to be able to take the annoyance, but you as chairman just can't stand it any longer. Step forward quickly, stop the speaker, and then addressing the yapping know-it-all, you say, "If Mr. Brasshead will only speak a bit louder we will all be able to hear what it is he is trying to tell Mr. Tinbeard." This will get a laugh if you don't appear to be angry. Brasshead and Tinbeard will keep quiet.

(2) What does a chairman do when the meeting is an exciting one, full of enthusiasm and everyone appears to want to talk at the same time? Remember that a noisy meeting can never be controlled by a shouting chairman. The thing to do is go along with the tide as you slowly begin to regain full control of the meeting. Stand in one place, in one position. Look quiet and be quiet. Make all your gestures and remarks deliberate. Talk to the persons nearest to you in a quiet tone. The ones in the rear will soon become curious and want to know what you are saying. They will quiet down quickly. As soon as you can be heard, make an appeal to their fair-mindedness. Don't scold. Ask for their cooperation. If the group is not set on sabotage or disruption, they will go along and you'll soon have order restored.

(3) When during a question or discussion period, several people rise simultaneously and begin shouting, you are faced with a problem that requires instantaneous reaction on your part. You must be the personification of strength. Wave the shouting members down. Steadily and firmly you demonstrate by gestures of the hands and arms that you will not

permit the meeting to go on and no questions or discussion will be permitted until order is restored. The excited members finally listen. Get in there fast. "If all of you will be patient, the Chair will recognize every one in due time. There will be no favoritism shown. Just be patient. The chairman recognizes the lady over there in the flower-pot hat. The rest will please be seated."

(4) Take another situation where the meeting becomes exciting. There are a number of persons on their feet anxious to take the speaker apart. He appears to be able to handle them all. Don't interfere. Move up behind the speaker and a little to the side. You are there to impress the audience with the fact that you are ready to back up the speaker if he should need help. As long as it does not get out of hand, let the speaker handle the excited questioners or hecklers. Your stepping in will only make matters worse. Sometimes the speaker deserves to be taken apart. Let the audience do it as long as they maintain order. Keep out of it.

As you gain more and more experience you will be more and more able to sense exactly what steps you must take.

Chapter 4

A FEW THOUSAND WORDS ON HUMOR

No MATTER how much has been written about humor and its importance to the human race, there is still as much more yet to be written, and even then the whole story will not have been told.

Humor is almost as important to life as air. It cannot substitute for air but it sure can make the air we breathe feel more delicious, more exhilarating, more joyful. What humor can do to air, it can do to many other things. If a newly married woman serves well-salted charcoal in place of that succulent filet mignon or that choice batch of oysters the husband brought home, is there anything that can more easily wash away the pains and pangs and hold back that male desire to commit mayhem or murder than a timely and appropriate bit of humor? Certainly not. (But the bride should make certain that the humor is there and on time and appropriate—there are no guarantees that go with this book.)

There is a time and a place for humor just as there is a time and place for almost everything in life. An attempt at humor at the wrong time can *give* a reaction that is as deadly as the user had hoped it would be warm. There is no rule which tells when humor is timely and when it is not. Humor may be timely and in place at a funeral, yet not timely nor in place at a discussion involving the art of selling shoelaces. When speaking before a group of hard-bitten serious-minded fundamentalists, it is best not to make any attempt at humor. A student group is usually ready for a touch of humor at any time.

In every situation there is room for humor—even if the humor is grim. Grim humor can best be defined as that humor which some chairmen try to use and murder in a shameful manner. This is only one definition. There are many more that are worse.

As has already been said—humor is a great asset and should be used wherever and whenever possible, provided (1) it is timely, (2) appropriate, and (3) does not impose upon the listeners (or readers).

Is humor always timely? No, it is not. There is always a certain point in the exchange of ideas that brings all minds to a psychological situation in which the weight of the problem is extraordinarily heavy.

Sometimes a group of normal happy people are confronted with a problem that has them all stumped. Every suggestion looking toward a solution has been turned down. Nothing but failure and disappointment can be foreseen. Mentally the individuals involved are slightly out of sorts. They feel helpless and frustrated. What they want is a solution to the troublesome problem. They want help. They are in no mood for humor of any kind. Under such circumstances humor is no longer humor and may even be considered sheer stupidity.

Whether or not a particular moment is timely is a matter of "feel." As a chairman you must get the "feel" of the situation. The feel requires a complete and thorough understanding of everything relating to the situation at hand. In sports, in entertainment, in publicity and a multitude of other endeavors the understanding is demonstrated by "timing," i.e., at the exact second a certain act is performed or a picture shown or a release issued. When the thing is "timed" right the results are good; and so it is with humor. There may be a proper type of audience and a good subject and everything else one may desire, but if the timing is not just right the humor will fall flat and boomerang.

Is the humor appropriate? In the law there is a doctrine known as "caveat emptor." Roughly translated, this means: "Let the buyer beware." The chairman is a seller and only in one way a buyer. He is selling himself to the audience and buying their good feelings. The chairman who does not know when his attempt at humor is appropriate would do well to remember the phrase "caveat emptor" because inappropriate attempts at humor will buy snickers, contempt, derision, hostility, revulsion, loss of interest, and even more violent reactions.

A situation in which a chairman was taught a good lesson occurred in a political rally of national importance in a major city of our country in 1944. After a great deal of effort on the part of many influential people, a political symposium was arranged in which two nationally publicized candidates appeared at the same time on the same platform to discuss a problem of great importance. A number of microphones were placed about the auditorium in anticipation of the question period. Everything was moving along very smoothly and all of the audience was evidently getting set for the real fireworks, when adherents of each of the speakers would fire loaded questions. The chairman for no reason whatsoever felt called upon to make some humorous remarks. He did. They were most inappropriate. The discussion between the candidates related to labor, the "humorous" story related to fish. There was hardly a chuckle in the audience. The situation was embarrassing and un-pleasant. Suddenly a female voice was heard over the loud-

(72)

speaker system. In a tone that left no mistake about her reaction to the chairman's inappropriate remarks she uttered two words: "That stinks." The chairman didn't dare try to stop the hysterical laughter. The audience in an instant realized that one of the microphones had been opened too soon; the lady didn't know it and thought she was whispering her sentiment to a friend nearby. Without intending to, she taught the chairman a lesson. Her succinct phrase spoke for all of them. Just as a chairman must feel that his humor is "timely" so he must know what is appropriate.

Generally speaking it will be found that humor which pokes fun at old people or persons with physical or mental defects of any kind is not well received. This is due to the fact that in our form of society such persons receive special protective treatment and any attack upon them calls up unfavorable reactions. Humor that is hard on women is also frowned upon. This does not mean that all humor about women is frowned upon. The type that is not appreciated is the type that makes them seem ridiculous. Feminists particularly get riled at such attempts at humor.

Humor should not impose upon the listeners. This is a matter of good taste and good manners on the chairman's part. Many persons do not like off-color stories or insinuating remarks, particularly those that have a sex angle to them. Avoid such humor and respect the feelings of the members in the audience who do not like it. Humor that pokes fun at groups must be handled very, very carefully. Referring to a member of a national group in slang or uncomplimentary terms is harsh and wrong and grates on the nerves of persons opposed to all forms of discrimination or bias. For example, a story relating to a Chinese person should never include the word "Chinaman" or "Chink"; an Irish person should never be referred to as a "Harp" or a

(73)

Japanese as a "Jap" Humor handled in this manner does impose on the audience.

The use of derisive terms or terms of mockery is resented more and more as time goes on. Intelligent people feel that they are being subjected to insults to their intelligence when a chairman or speaker has to use such terms as "Chink" for a Chinese or "Harp" for an Irishman or "Dago" for an Italian in an attempt at humor. There are many other such terms. None of them are acceptable. They should be avoided.

What may be said of group references may also be said about references to known individuals. Where the humor holds them up to ridicule or shame or in any way casts doubt or aspersions upon the person's character, fictitious names should be used. (Keep in mind possible slander actions.)

When a chairman knows of something humorous about a speaker, it is perfectly proper for the chairman to tell about it, provided that it does not hold the speaker up to ridicule or make him appear stupid. A good-natured joke on the speaker is all right and even helps get him across to the audience. As a general rule it is safe to tell humorous stories about a speaker. With a few exceptions, they are always helpful. If the humorous story is flattering to the speaker, that's always in order.

Humor is one instrument that every chairman should use to relieve a tense situation. Sometimes an unfortunate argument may ensue between two speakers. The air is surcharged with ill feeling—this is the time when a chairman who knows how to be a good chairman can come in with his humor at the right time with something that is appropriate. That which helps dispel the feeling of hostility and restores good will is appropriate.

A word about who may not attempt to be humorous.

There are some persons who make good chairmen. They know what to do and how to do it and when to do it, but they just aren't funny. Such an individual should never forget that his is not the personality that fits into the groove for chairmen who can handle humor. If in doubt don't try to be funny. You may wind up appearing ridiculous.

The following is an excellent example of what a good chairman can do with humor when properly handled. A careful study of every word in the article will fully reward the reader.

BESIDE THE POINT*

When we first read an Associated Press dispatch in January, about paper-tearing birds in England we didn't pay much attention, though the account was, in its way, hair-raising. A long-named ornithologist, Lieutenant-Colonel W. M. Logan Home, who was investigating the matter, said that he had had letters from 2,000 persons reporting the depredations of birds identified as blue tits. The little blue devils had swooped into houses and torn paper off the walls, mangled leather photograph frames, ripped clothes off lines and pecked off the tops of milk bottles —they drank the milk.

Now comes the news, in another A. P. dispatch, that rooks, jackdaws, bullfinches, and magpies have joined the blue tits in the anti-paper campaign, and even as we write are making furious assaults on books, stray newspapers, bus tickets, pamphlets, and milk-bottle tops.

According to the British Trust for Ornithology, up to 1949 there were only eighty-seven reports of paper-tearing, with earliest observations going back to 1904, but the movement has grown prodigiously during the past year.

* "Beside the Point," by Robert Bendiner and Margaret Marshall. Reprinted by special permission from *The Nation* of July 15, 1950.

It is not clear, as yet, whether this is a left-wing or a right-wing uprising or what its ultimate aim may be. What is clear is that the blue tits are good organizers and have an effective propaganda line.

Experienced observers from the *New Statesman* and the London School of Economics are not surprised that the blue tits should have appealed, by their violent methods, to irresponsible elements like magpies, who enjoy destruction for its own sake; but the fact that they have also been able to enlist such respectable birds as bullfinches is worrying the authorities, especially since the Orme-Kysow-Dowton incident of May 13, which was also reported here by the A.P.

In the London suburb of Ealing that day a bird power-dived and snatched the spectacles off the nose of C. J. Orme; a moment later the same bird, presumably, pounced on William Kysow and seized his spectacles; and then it was revealed that, a few days before, Eric Dowton had been subjected to a similar attack, which had failed.

On this occasion the Royal Society for the Prevention of Cruelty to Animals and Owls—that's what the dispatch called it—got to work. An inspector set an owl trap and baited it with a pocket mirror. The culprit was caught and did in fact turn out to be a barn owl. The owl was pronounced mad, which is what people in Western democracies always say about such characters, but shrewd observers saw in the affair evidence that the blue tits have persuaded the wisest of birds to join their ranks. According to this view, the Ealing barn owl, in his fanatical zeal, was collecting spectacles for the use of a triumvirate of big-time owls who may be directing the movement and must stay up till all hours of the day reading the books, newspapers, and pamphlets captured by the cadres, or raiding parties.

As we indicated before, the ultimate aim of the movemert is not clear. Our own theory is that the flying squadrons are out to eliminate paper work of all kinds and that the A.P. will shortly have big news for us—namely, that an overpowering army of birds has swooped into Whitehall and denuded the government offices of letters in triplicate, memoranda, records-going-back-to-1350, and reports—preliminary, interim, and final. After that anything may happen. A Kamikaze owl may even try to snatch the spectacles off Stafford Cripps.

Meanwhile there is a shred of evidence that the organization has agents in this country. (The first A.P. dispatch pointed out, ominously, that the blue tits are cousins to American chickadees.) The other day in Deal, New Jersey, Robert Bertelsen stopped short to avoid stepping on what looked like an innocent bird pecking at the ground. Mr. Bertelsen stumbled, lurched, and broke a plate-glass window of the service station he works for—it cost him nine dollars.

You can't tell us, alerted as we are by the Assiduous Press, that that bird didn't do it on purpose. He obviously wanted the glass broken so his gang could swoop in and tear up the waiting list for new cars, thereby throwing the community into turmoil and panic and possibly civil strife. It's an old revolutionary trick. The bird escaped, of course, and the Federal Bird Investigators (F.B.I.) have not yet been able to identify or locate the troublemaker.

From now on we're going to be very wary of birds in general. As for the pigeons that are always hanging around our office window, we'll watch them like a hawk. They are probably out to *"get"* the copy for this column.

(If they succeed, we'll at least know how to interpret, the next time we hear it, the hoot of an owl.) M.M.

Chapter 5

HOW TO PLAN A MASS MEETING

IN A DEMOCRACY the people are free to gather together to agitate for or against any proposition. If none or very few are concerned about a particular situation, there is no likelihood of any mass meeting or meetings being held. The term speaks for itself. It is a meeting of a mass of people. This mass of people is not of one mind on everything. The mass is not of one mind on anything. All the mass has in common is an unorganized idea about a given broad subject. All the people in a given locality are anxious to have their community stand out as the cleanest, the safest, the best administered, etc. Can it be said that all those who gather together at a mass meeting to protest against an alarming increase in accidents in the town are thinking along the same lines about how properly to handle the situation? Definitely not. Some want more policemen patrolling all the streets, others want the Traffic Bureau to be more stringent in enforcing the traffic laws, and still another group has a third idea, and so on and on and on.

That which applies to a mass meeting relating to safety also applies to a mass meeting relating to street cleanliness, the elimination of graft in public office, or anything else.

There have been in the past many mass meetings for the purpose of protesting against barbaric acts on the part of the cruder elements in our society. A number of years ago

(78)

two unfortunate gentlemen known as Sacco and Vanzetti were unjustly arrested, jailed, and eventually put to death by the State of Massachusetts. The consciences of millions of decent-minded citizens were aroused at the idea that two innocent men were to die because the Commonwealth of Massachusetts was too cowardly to admit its shameful error. Mass meetings were held all over the United States of America and other parts of the world. Did these mass meetings all do the same thing or say exactly the same thing even though they were all called because of this grave miscarriage of justice? They did not. Each meeting in its own way tried to express its anger and the feeling of horror at what was about to take place. Some passed resolutions, some offered prayers. A large number sent telegrams of protest and many by *viva voce* (voice) vote decided to appeal to the President of the United States.

All of them were mass meetings in every sense of the word. One big idea for all with a large number of ways and means of dramatizing the thoughts around the idea.

To give an example of how to get a mass meeting going, we shall suppose a hypothetical situation as follows:

For a number of years the area in which we live has been growing at a very rapid pace. Five years ago there were 1,000 children of school age; there were 20,000 inhabitants and 3,500 homes. The school was built to accommodate comfortably 800-900 children. The police department was adequate for all purposes and so were other branches of local government.

Some five years ago a large public development in the field of atomic research was started about three miles out of town. The public development together with the businesses that sprang up has increased our school population to the extent that there are now 3,500 school children; 4,000

(79)

people have been added to our community; and hundreds upon hundreds of new houses have been built. Conditions are appalling, but the city fathers refuse to do much about it. Their attitude is: "It was good enough for us and it will have to be good enough for the newcomers." Mothers and other progressive-minded citizens have pleaded with the mayor and city council but all to no avail. Things keep going from bad to worse. A small group is determined that the city of Squelch is going to do the right thing by the people. Something must be done! The group meets in the home of Hugh R. Stuck to talk things over. Says Mr. Stuck: "As long as we go about trying to do things each by himself or herself we are not going to get very far. We've got to get all the people together and see to it that the boys in City Hall get off those cane seats and do the right thing."

"How can we do that?" asks Mrs. Timidfoot. "If there's work to be done you can count on me," says Mr. Puffer. "My kid almost got run over on his way home from school because there was no cop at the crossing." "What are we to do with the garbage these days?" is the question Mrs. Squareface wants answered.

"O.K. now, folks," says Mr. Stuck. "We all have complaints. There are not enough schools, we need fifty more teachers, about a half dozen or more playgrounds. There should be more firemen, health inspectors, building inspectors, more sanitation department equipment and employees. There are a number of things that must be done. I suggest the following first.

"(1) List all the grievances we have. Not imaginary ones or personal gripes but the kind that affect us all. Everybody get a pencil and paper and write everything down. (2) When that has been done we'll take the next step. We'll all become members of a Committee for the Redress of Grievances in the city of Squelch. This committee will sift through all the grievances and set them up in a list. (3) We'll call a mass meeting and demand that the mayor and the city council come and hear what we have to say. How does that strike you?" asks Mr. Stuck.

Everyone is silent for a few moments and then Mrs. Timid-foot inquires: "How do you do all the things you are talking about, Mr. Stuck?" "Very simple, very simple," he answers them, "all I want to know is whether you are with me." All those present chime in with a chorus of "sures" and "yeses." Mr. Stuck takes over.

Now the first thing we must do is agree that we are all going to work together as a committee. We are going to choose a chairman, a secretary, and a treasurer for this committee. The chairman will preside at committee meetings and be the guiding hand. The secretary will keep a record of everything that happens at committee meetings, answer all inquiries, send out notices and letters, etc., and keep all the records. All too frequently the job of secretary goes to someone with a neat writing hand or the first person who shows a fountain pen or pencil. This is wrong—very wrong. A secretary is an important person performing an important function. It is the secretary who writes down, for all and sundry to read when necessary, everything that has occurred. It is bad practice to rely on the memory of any man or men. That which is written down can always be re-examined, whereas the memory can be poor, uncertain, and even influenced by outside stimuli (yes, even honestly so). The secretary who knows what to do writes down every action taken. He or she does not bother with arguments for or against a given motion or proposal. Arguments are not actions. Many persons say things without thinking, therefore it is not important for a secretary to make note of argu-

(81)

ments. Take this example: It is voted to appropriate $100.00 to send a delegation of three members to see the governor of the state about the dishonest local officials. Is it important to tell who argued in what vein or manner for or against the motion? No, it is not important. The important things are $100.00, three members in a delegation, and the visit to the governor about the dishonest local officials. What the secretary writes down in the regular course of business at a meeting can be used in suits at law— that is how important the secretary's job is. If the secretary's records show that the notes were written by a person of intelligence and that the notes appear to be carefully taken, the Court is impressed much more favorably than by notes that contain a lot of immaterial gibberish. But this is not all that a good secretary does. Letters must be answered. Care must be taken to say the right thing. Peoples' feelings must not be hurt and the rights and property and dignity of the organization must be protected. Who does all this? A good secretary.

Members must be notified about meetings. They must be given exact information as to time and place. The secretary does this. Reminders to committee chairmen to do this or that by a certain date. Again, it's the secretary who does all this. Yes, the secretary's job is a hard but interesting one. It has its headaches and heartaches but it also has its compensations and happy moments.

The treasurer will be responsible for all money taken in or paid out. A word or two about treasurers. This office is one that requires a meticulous individual—that is, one who will see to it that there is a receipt for every penny spent as well as every penny taken in. If there is the slightest doubt about the disposition of funds, the beginning of trouble is firmly planted in the organization. A good treasurer has

(82)

bills for all purchases made. If it is impossible to get bills, then a complete memorandum should be made. When members find that at any time it is possible to ask about the money received and how it has been spent or being protected, the members will have much more faith in the organization and be more willing to lend a helping hand. It is not the amount of money unaccounted for that drives members away but the idea that there is one in their midst in whom they have placed their trust, and it has been betrayed. This always causes members to lose heart. Remember, then, that a good treasurer is like a good home—which always has a feeling of warmth and security and strength about it.

There will be assistants for each of these officers and there will also be a division of work, but in each case the secretary or the treasurer is primarily responsible for the acts of the assistants.

When all of the grievances have been properly listed and set down we will get up some literature. That's the second thing to do. One or two members of the committee will write a leaflet or a small pamphlet telling briefly about the things that are not being done and the need that exists. In these days when democracy is on trial and every believer in democracy is duty bound to put his shoulder to the wheel, it is well to remember that the destiny of this country was once steered by certain pamphleteers and leaflet writers. Remember Ben Franklin, Tom Paine, and Sam Adams? What a wonderful thing it would be if, instead of inane untrue jingles over the air and misleading "ads" in newspapers or magazines, the citizens of our country were bombarded with leaflets and pamphlets—well written and setting forth the facts. No dictatorially minded fascists could lead our people toward goals that end only in the abyss of misery and disappointment. Facts are what we need to know and they will guide us to the right goal. As soon as that is arranged for, we must begin to think about money. The third thing to do, then, is to begin collecting money. In almost every case of a mass meeting's being arranged, the first money is put up by the organizing committee. That is part of the price we pay for liberty and democracy. The committee members will each advance a small sum of money until the full committee is functioning. When funds are available all advances must be returned.

Members should know that they are safe in placing their trust in the organization and its representatives. If members are asked to make loans to the organization on the promise that the money will be returned out of the first funds received, then by all means keep faith with the trusting members. Keeping faith builds up confidence; *it* builds up credit; it builds up morale. When members know that their loans will be repaid, they will not hesitate to come forward on every occasion to help out financially. There are many people who belong to organizations but do nothing in the form of activity. When they get the chance to lend money to the group it salves their conscience, but even they do not want to lose their money. These same persons will be more and more eager to help out financially if they find that they have not been fooled. It is good to have such backers. Cultivate them. Remember. Return all loans made by members.

Thus far the following has been accomplished: (1) It has been agreed that a committee shall be formed. (2) The committee shall have a chairman, a secretary, and a treasurer. (3) The committee will start analyzing the purposes for which it was formed. (4) The need for literature is recognized and someone is to be put in charge of that phase

(84)

of the work. (5) Money is to be made available for the committee's immediate needs.

We return again to the home of Mr. Stuck and follow the proceedings a bit more.

Mr. Stuck: "We are not the only people in this city who are interested in our problems. There are many organizations that would surely wish to be represented on a committee such as ours. There are parent-teacher associations, civic clubs, businessmen's associations, religious groups, fraternal groups, trade unions, etc. We must get a list of all of them. Send each one a letter telling about our meeting and invite all of them to send representatives to our next meeting or to let us know when their representatives can attend if our meeting night is not to their liking. Be very careful and tell them that ours is a *temporary* organizing committee, that all plans made to date are only tentative, and that final plans will be made after all those who are interested have had a full opportunity to be heard. Remember that intelligent civic-minded persons do not like the idea of coming into any situation where everything is cut and dried and they are merely 'yes' men."

The temporary committee now gets down to the business of preparing to do two more things. One: make a list of all organizations that may possibly be interested. Two: communicate with all of them and invite their participation.

There is a third thing to be done by the temporary committee: sending representatives to appear before the different organizations and speak at their meetings. The value and importance of this activity can never be too strongly emphasized. Most organizations function through an executive committee between business meetings. The executive committees generally meet at regular stated intervals and it is not too difficult to get permission to appear and be heard. If the representative of the temporary organizing committee is a presentable and intelligent individual the chances are that the executive committee will include the request of the temporary committee representative in the minutes that are eventually read to the membership. In some instances the executive committee has joined with the organizing committee even though the general membership has had no opportunity to vote on the proposal. This is done when the executive committee feels certain that the membership will agree to go along or where there will not be time enough to submit the matter to the membership. Choose the individual who is to appear before other organizations with the following qualifications in mind: (1) Appearance. It is first impressions that count for a great deal. The fellow who looks like a Milquetoast may prove more brilliant in the long run, but in this case there is only a short time and we must strike while the iron is hot. (2) Ability to put across the idea. Without this characteristic there is virtually no chance of success. The fellow who cannot put the idea across cannot be of much help. (3) A well-known individual. If the organization is fortunate enough to enlist the aid of an individual or individuals who are well known, the battle is more than three-quarters won. (4) If possible, get a member of the organization being visited to do the job. If there is a choice between two or more persons having approximately the same qualifications and one is a member of the organization to be visited, choose the member. He is presumed to know his way about more easily, will meet with less opposition, and can argue from the point of view of his own organization.

It is axiomatic that no one is ever sent as a representative of an organizing committee to an organization where such

(86)

representative is hostile to the organization being visited. For example, don't send a rabid atheist to a church group or an employer who has a strike in his plant to a trade union. The point is simple.

In addition to representatives going to visit organizations to enlist their aid, there is another piece of important work to be done. It is called public relations. A good public relations man or woman knows how to get across to the general public the idea back of the mass meeting being planned. Public relations men and women get a hearing on radio and television as well as notices in newspapers and magazines and in some instances have even been able to enlist the aid of the motion picture groups. The public relations man or woman is a combination of many things. He is a good fellow and well liked. He is everywhere all the time but is not an obnoxious pusher. If he "puts one over" it is considered clever and part of his business—any other citizen would be considered a boor. The public relations man makes palatable and interesting that which otherwise might be considered questionable and distasteful. The public relations man is the fellow who gets the grouchy police chief to think it's a good idea to have a torchlight parade on a busy Saturday night. You see now what is meant by a public relations and publicity man. A good one is worth his weight in gold.

At this point we find that the temporary organizing committee has done all it can possibly do, and we must await further developments. The notices have gone out, the different organizations have been contacted by a representative of the temporary committee (in addition to the letter that was sent), and the date for the meeting of the full committee which includes delegates or representatives from interested organizations has been set.

This does not mean that the committee members sit down

and twiddle their thumbs. On the contrary. They use every opportunity to publicize their activities. They write more letters and still more. They scout about for new personalities and additional organizations. Not until the very last second do they let up in their expanding activities. Let's look in and see what happens.

The meeting is called to order by Mr. Stuck. Very briefly he tells all those assembled what the reasons are for the contemplated mass meeting and about all the events leading up to the present meeting. He says: "Everything that was done may be changed around by the will of the majority of the assembled groups. This is the democratic way of doing things. Fascists, Nazis, and Communists do not do things this way. Those who believe in democracy do. Therefore it is up to those present to decide finally what is to be done."

The secretary, Mrs. Timidfoot, reads the names of all the organizations that have been invited, their responses if any, the names of their representatives if any, and also letters or other communications received.

The treasurer, Mr. Puffer, gives a report of the money he received, the amount he expended and the bills therefor, and the amount on hand and where it is being kept. He turns over the bills to the secretary. The treasurer's account must show what has been done with every penny received.

Mr. Stuck takes over again. The assembled individuals are asked to express their opinion about going forward with the proposed plans. They favor doing so. Now a permanent chairman, secretary, and treasurer are to be chosen. When this has been done and a permanent committee chosen, the time and place for the coming mass meeting are set. In addition, preparations must be made for speakers. (See Chapter 2 about getting speakers.) Well-known names are preferable. Big shots, authorities in different fields—those are the speakers to go after.

The mass meeting is called to impress the mayor and city council. A resolution must be prepared in proper form. The resolution must contain a recital of all the grievances promulgated by the committee. At the end of the resolution an invitation in the form of a request to the mayor and city council to attend and hear should be included. If the citizens are well enough organized the request may be in the form of a demand. Unfortunately some public officials do not understand refined terminology. They must be commanded as they command their underlings. This done, we now turn our attention to another matter.

The work to be done should be spread out among as many members as can possibly be involved. Keep the interest up by keeping everyone busy. Cut down the talkers and help along the workers. In every organization there are glory birds. Clip their wings and pluck their feathers if they don't work. The problem of members who just belong is found in every organization. The discovery of this fact frequently causes trouble when active members raise their voices in protest over the lazy attitude of the shirkers. To make matters even worse, some of the most enthusiastic and hard-working members become discouraged over the attitude of the indifferent ones. There is no all-inclusive answer to this problem. Sometimes the activities of members around them shame the shirkers into activity. Frequently the active members snub the inactive ones and make sure that the undeserving pieces of dead wood are kept away from any of the pleasanter tasks that may be part of the organization's work.

Just one more thing. When a mass meeting is being held,

be sure to arrange the seating on the platform so that every representative of every organization is given full recognition. Put all their names on all the literature. Don't pull a faux pas and cause unnecessary friction. Be thorough, thoughtful, and diplomatic. No detail is too small to be attended to; a good mass meeting can do in one full swoop more than hundreds of petitions. Use this technique to further democracy.

In choosing a man or woman to run the chair, pick one who has demonstrated an ability to take over and handle the chair with absolute confidence. If a big-name chairman is available who can do a good job, that is a good thing. On the other hand, if a little-known person is known as a very good chairman, by all means take the competent little-known citizen, in preference to the incompetent "big shot."

Mass meetings are demonstrations of democracy in action. The bigger they are, the better for us. All of us.

Chapter 6

PLANNING AND RUNNING A POLITICAL FORUM

THE PEOPLE of our country are still strongly interested in political forums. In some places the home folks get such a thrill out of good verbal battles during the election campaigns that they discuss them for months and even years thereafter—and, not infrequently, the stories that are retold are less than half true. Be that as it may, a red-hot political fight is almost second to none as a long-lasting thriller.

One of the component parts of a sizzling campaign is the political forum. There is a big difference between a political forum and a one-sided political meeting. The forum is what we are after.

Maybe you've heard this before, but it will bear repeating. ALWAYS BE SURE TO PLAN YOUR FORUM. Plans bring good results in 99 out of 100 cases.

Rule 1: *Always plan your forum about 6 to 8 weeks in advance.* This is not too long or too short a period of time. Bear in mind that political parties generally plan their important events much in advance of the actual date of occurrence. Therefore *give* yourself the 6 to 8 weeks' time so that you can fit your plans into the schedule of all the political parties.

As the campaign advances, the number of open dates of each candidate grows less and less and the chances of corralling the candidate grow more and more unlikely. Thus, if * you make your request for certain speakers early enough, you stand a good chance of getting the ones you want.

Rule 1A. *Start your plan by setting dates.* This is important because it gives the yardstick by which all activity can be gauged. For example, a committee that is charged with the responsibility of getting out printed matter knows in advance what dates must be set as deadlines for the different phases of activity. The committee can tell the printer that only a given number of days or weeks may be taken by him to do a given job. The pressure of time that makes itself felt by the printing committee also makes its mark on all other committees. Timing is important.

Rule IB. *Pick a place for the forum.* Political forums should be held in meeting places that have long traditions attached to them. If many of the oldtimers talk about Beelzebub Hall, with a far-away look in their eyes and a voice that quivers with reverence, then you can bet that the musty old walls that entomb the mob in Beelzebub Hall will bring them back again. Politics may be dirty, but dirty old halls don't spoil political forums.

Are schools out of bounds? No, no, no. Schools may be good places to meet provided that the school is a popular place. If, through the years, the school has been the scene of many meetings that have been successful, then by all means you may use the school. When much of the local pride revolves around the exploits of the football or basketball squad of the school, you have a good meeting place. Remember that in the last analysis you know best where to meet. This rule is a general one but it need not always be followed. Ninety percent of the time is good enough.

Rule 1C. *Get started immediately on your publicity.* You have the time, the place, and the subject matter—get going on the publicity. A person or persons with ideas will always get good publicity. Start in low gear. A short announcement to the press—all of the papers in the area. Something that very succinctly tells the whole story: "The Executive Committee of Watertight Valley Civic Association, at its meeting last night, set aside Friday evening February 30th, at Beelzebub Hall, as the occasion for an all-party political forum on the campaign issues in this election. All top candidates are being invited to take part in this exciting biennial event. Ethel Eggs Sec'y·" This is just the kind of newspaper release that stands a chance of being published. It tells much in little space. It embraces something in which many people are interested. Columns that contain short notices of events to come are always on the look-out for such information. To all political clubs, social clubs, community clubs, etc., a short letter should be sent. This first letter is not an invitation. It is a notice; the beginning of a stream of publicity. In some cities and towns the radio stations will pass on the information to their listeners during off-hours or on programs conducted by well-known personalities. Announcements of events to come are made frequently on such programs in New York City as "Around New York" over WNYC, "This is New York" over WCBS with Bill Leonard, over WOR by Martha Deane, and on occasion Alma Dettinger over WQXR in "Other Peoples' Business." These are only a few of the radio programs that can be approached. In almost every town or city there are similar personalities and radio events. None of them are difficult to approach. In the majority of instances the real persons are as interesting and charming as they sound over the air. A little note to the individual you wish to reach and you may generally feel sure that he or she will help. If he is too busy with program work, he will invariably have a well-trained assistant to lend a willing hand. Try it and you'll be very much surprised by the good results.

Rule ID. *Use leaflets only when your forum is aimed at attracting local interest only.* There is no need to waste a great deal of time and energy if the forum you are planning is going to attract the people in the immediate neighborhood only. In such cases you slant all your efforts toward an effective contact campaign by leaflet distribution and announcements in neighborhood stores and gathering places. Suppose you live in the town or village of X, which is 25 miles from the village of Y. Would it be wise to spend time plugging the newspapers in the village of Y with press releases, announcements, leaflets, etc.? Frankly speaking, no. Set the geographical limits in which you are going to work and then figure out how many persons there are to contact. Gather as large a group as you can and divide the job of spreading the information about the coming forum. Remember what was said in a previous chapter about telephone calls, personal invitations, etc. Repeat that technique here. Suppose you don't know many of the people, what then? So what! Members of the group that is running the big event knock at strangers' doors and follow somewhat this routine. "Good evening, sir, I just want to invite you to come to the big political forum at Beelzebub Hall on February 30. All the parties are going to be there. You'll enjoy it and we will be glad to have you. Here's a reminder. ..." With a handful of conscientious members a great deal of territory can be covered. Handbills distributed in this manner do a lot of good. When handed out to passersby, figure on a one or two percent return. Only in exceptional cases is the percentage ever higher. Chances are pretty good that the results will be better than expected. People respect civic-minded citizens. Even if they don't come, they will at

(94)

least have heard about the event and in conversation with others may mention it favorably. All to the good, friend, all to the good.

Rule IE. *Use newspaper ads if you can afford them.* Barring morons, the ultra-literate, and the busy clothes horses, most people read newspapers. Maybe they're not worth reading but most of us do it just the same. It's sort of a habit.

If the treasury can stand it, a good-sized ad once or twice a week makes success almost certain. Add to this, three or four ads the last few days before the forum takes place and you can sit back full of confidence.

When the organization works on a budget so thin that it is transparent, you have a different problem. Put in a modest ad once a week. This is a great help. Take pains in *getting* up the ad and check carefully with the paper to be sure it gets a conspicuous spot. When the budget can support only one ad, throw it all into a blurb one or two days before the great crisis. Make it hit just the right spot at the right time. Let's take a look back. We now have time, place, publicity, and advertising. Is that all? Oh no! Not so easy.

Rule IF. *Some responsible person should be given the task of getting accurate data.* This includes: (a) the full and correct names of the candidates who are to appear; (b) the correct political party; (c) full and correct biographical data, obtained from the candidate himself whenever possible; (d) the office the candidate is campaigning for; (e) if women are involved, be careful to ascertain whether the title is Mrs. or Miss. When a woman is a widow, she *is* referred to as Mrs. Mary Squelch and not Mrs. Jonathan Strongarm Squelch.

Write or telephone to the prospective speakers and check * with them the accuracy of the biographical sketch given;

also make certain that you get the correct spelling and pronunciation of the name of the candidate and the organization to which he belongs. There have been many instances in which the mispronunciation of a speaker's name has resulted in a great deal of embarrassment and, in some instances, has caused unnecessary hard feeling. These are very simple rules to remember and should always be borne in mind.

Rule 2. *In the time elapsing between the planning of the meeting and the actual event, committee members should "scout" the speakers.* That is, a committee member should be assigned to attend a meeting at which the prospective speaker is appearing. The committee member should make notes from a strictly objective point of view and rate the speaker in the following manner:

(1) (a) Poor on delivery and unintelligent
     (b) Poor on delivery but well informed
     (c) Poor on delivery but confused
(2) (a) Fair in delivery but unintelligent
     (b) Fair in delivery and well informed
     (c) Fair in delivery but confused
(3) (a) Good on delivery but unintelligent as to subject matter
     (b) Good on delivery and well informed
     (c) Good on delivery but confused as to subject
(4) (a) Excellent on delivery but unintelligent — just oratory
     (b) Excellent on delivery and well informed
     (c) Excellent on delivery but confused as to subject matter.

The weakest speaker is heard first. This, of course, is not " always possible. Unfortunately, some persons who are poor speakers hold important positions in the community. They

(96)

must be given a good spot on the program. Generally speaking, however, the poorest speaker opens the program. Another exception to the rule is the use of a good speaker at the beginning of the program in order to "pep up" the meeting. Each meeting, of course, has its particular problems, and arrangements must be modified to meet such problems.

The above-mentioned rule is generally accepted, but it is not an iron-clad one.

A poor speaker is followed by either another poor speaker or a fair one. Under no circumstances whatsoever should more than two poor speakers follow one another. Naturally, if all the speakers are poor, the organizing committee has no choice in the matter. Goodness knows, the crop of poor speakers outnumbers the good speakers ten to one.

When the chairman of the evening finds that the poor speaker was so bad that to follow him with another poor speaker would result in a stampede for the exits, then the chairman should use his own discretion and soften the agony by throwing into the breach a good speaker.

ALWAYS TRY TO KEEP YOUR BEST SPEAKER FOR THE END. That leaves the audience with a feeling of excitement and pleasure. They will come back on another occasion. If the first two speakers are poor, the next speaker, whenever possible, must be at least rated good. He must have some of the qualities of a good speaker, a fine command of the language, a delightful sense of humor, an extraordinary personality, or a most impressive and clear manner of thinking. He simply *must* have one or more of these characteristics.

As was said before, if the gods are with the meeting, and there is one of those rare objects known as an excellent speaker, he (or she) is the wind-up man. Be sure to save enough time for him so that he can make up for all of the things the audience was compelled to suffer.

Speakers should be told exactly when they are expected to arrive. They should be taken into the secret of when the meeting will actually begin. Each speaker should be told how many speakers will precede and follow him, how much time is to be allotted to each one, and whether or not there will be a question-and-answer period.

All organizations that run political forums have learned by experience that it is most unwise to give one organization more time than another. The audience resents it when one group is treated better than another, even though the audience may not agree with the point of view of the mistreated group. Thus, if political parties A, B, C, D, and E have sent speakers and A, B, and C are allowed twenty minutes each, and parties D and E are allotted less time, the audience will condemn such treatment.

At the beginning of the meeting, the chairman should announce the amount of time allotted for speaking. He should also announce that there will be a signal at the five-minute period before concluding remarks are to be made; at the two-minute period before the concluding remarks must be made; and just before going into the final stretch. At the appointed time, the chairman should cut the speaker off. *The chairman must be firm.* He must treat *all* speakers alike. They soon learn to respect a chairman who knows his business and acts in an impartial manner.

The organization conducting the meeting should make it clear that it does or does not have a particular point of view politically. If the organization denies having a particular point of view, this should be stated by the chairman. The chairman must scrupulously observe the rules of impartiality and not indulge in subtle innuendoes or sly remarks.

(98)

Always remember that someone in the audience is just as bright as the chairman and, in some instances, may be even brighter. A docile audience can be whipped into almost a riotous mood by the undiplomatic actions of a chairman.

Always treat all speakers with the same consideration. The chairman must never begin to glow over the prospect of introducing a speaker who is the best this, the greatest that, and the most expert so and so, and one beloved by all, and. then follow such an introduction by a limp, dead-pan, uninteresting reference to the unfortunate individual who comes after the reborn Cicero.

Seating an audience is an act in itself. The care with which a meeting has been planned is always reflected to a large degree by the manner in which the audience is seated. Take as an example an auditorium divided into a central part, a right and a left section. Rope off all of the right and all of the left section as well as the rear half of the middle section. Leave about 100 or 150 seats open. As the people continue to come in and fill up the seats that are unroped, the ushers stand by to make more and more space available. All these precautions are not necessary when it is known in advance that there will be a full attendance.

There is a feeling of warmth in any meeting in which the audience is seated close together. When only 150 people attend a meeting in an auditorium that seats 750, the feeling of failure or of being let down is never so great when the 150 people are all seated in one area as when they are scattered all over the place. The speakers can block out the vacant seats when they can see a compact group of human beings in a specified area. Talking to a scattered group gives the speaker a reaction something similar to what a bowler gets when he has a second ball with which to knock down four remaining pins on different parts of the alley. He hopes

(99)

that by some fortunate twist of the ball the head of one pin will strike the base of another and both together will somehow come in contact with the remaining two pins. When the speaker sees heads scattered to the right, to the left, and in front of him, he is in a quandary about which side to favor. How is he going to get his voice to hit one side, bounce off the peoples' heads, and duly impress the scattered ones on the other two sides? It's not a good feeling for either audience or speaker. Remember then: bunch your people and you'll help make the meeting a successful one. With very little change in procedure, a forum of businessmen, church groups, or any other unit can be arranged.

Chapter 7

DEBATES, PANEL DISCUSSIONS, AND CONFERENCES

THE TERM "debate" is used to designate formal and informal discussions between persons having differences of opinion on a given subject. It appears to be a popular form of indoor sport not only in America but all over the world. Whenever men are free to get together and differ, there we find them engaging in debate. Sometimes the debate is deliberate, as in the Congress of the United States, and sometimes it comes about by accident. Our discussion will be limited to the debate that is deliberately brought on.

THE INFORMAL DEBATE

The first form of debate is the informal. A topic is chosen by an organization for discussion. The topic must be controversial in nature and subject to different interpretations. For example: "Euthanasia should be permitted by law." This subject of course is capable of two opposite points of view, and two or more speakers on opposite sides can easily be procured. Now we have the controversial subject. We go to the next step, which is getting two speakers—one for and one against. The first place to look for a speaker against the subject is the local or state medical society. Up to the present time the medical associations have been opposed to euthanasia. This is true of the national medical associations as well as all state and local associations. Now we must get a speaker for the proposition. The most likely place to find such a one is to ask "The Society for the Adoption of Euthanasia" or some other such group. If no one group can be found that concentrates on attaining this end, then we must turn our efforts to other groups. To do this most effectively, follow the suggestions found in Chapter 2. We shall assume that our efforts have resulted in our obtaining two speakers. All the preliminary work of setting the date and the place and getting all the committee members to function has been taken care of. See Chapter 1 for all the details.

This is the evening (or afternoon) of the debate. We skip over what was or should have been done. Mr. Smooth is the chairman. He has introduced the opponents to each other and has discussed the time allotted to each one. There will be a warning signal at the five-minute mark, the two-minute mark, the half-minute mark, and the signal to stop. The first speaker is for the proposition. He is to have 25 minutes for his opening presentation. His opponent is to have 30 minutes. The first speaker is then allowed 10 minutes for rebuttal and the matter can either be considered closed or there can be one of two alternatives, (a) The speakers may question each other, with the right to sum up for 5 minutes at the end. If this is done the proponent speaks first and the opponent speaks last, (b) Both speakers are subjected to questioning by the audience and summaries are permitted by both speakers, each summary being 5 minutes, and again the proponent speaks first. There are no judges and no decision as to who was the winner of the debate. The audience is the judge and each member makes his respective decision.

(102)

THE FORMAL DEBATE

Here we have a procedure that is set by formal rules. Generally two or more persons take opposite sides of a question. They function as teams—the proponents and the opponents of a given proposition. The question to be debated is put in the form of a resolution, such as the following: "RESOLVED: That euthanasia is beneficial to mankind."

The formal type of debate is popular in high schools and colleges and some very few debating societies. It is stilted in form and is not well adapted for the purpose of giving information objectively. It is a battle of wits in which logic and sometimes sophistry are used to attempt to color the presentation of the facts. Formal debates are "judged" by a judge or panel of judges who make their decision on a number of thing such as delivery, marshaling of facts, reasoning in rebuttal, etc.

A debater does not yield to persuasion. It is his job to stick to one point of view and try to convince the judges that his and his teammates' point of view is correct. The rules as to time allowed for presentation of main argument rebuttal and sur-rebuttal are all set in advance by national and international debating societies. If your organization is to have a formal debate, the best thing to do is to inquire of the debating society what their formal rules are and be guided accordingly.

The term "debate" has been applied to discussions between legislators in the halls of congresses and parliaments. In this type of debate the question of proponents and opponents is generally decided by the political philosophy of the member's party. He may find himself arguing against what he believes in his own mind just because the "bigwigs" in his party have decided that that is the more expedient tack to take. It is true that there are opposing sides; but a political compromise may result in amendments that resolve all differences and no opposing side exists any longer.

PANEL DISCUSSION

A panel discussion is one in which a group of persons foregather to discuss one subject, with each individual giving his or her particular point of view. The points of view coincide in the main, but the reasons for certain conclusions and the manner in which they are reached may differ widely. The panel discussion differs from the debate in that the speakers do not take opposite sides from the very outset as the debaters do. The participants in the panel limit their remarks to fit into the framework of the question at hand. For example: A panel discussion on "The United States of America and its Relationship with and to the Far East." Here we have a broad subject. There is no doubt about the fact that there is a relationship between the two geographical and political areas. How is it handled and what methods are used ?

In deciding upon the panel that is to discuss the topic above, as many persons from different walks of life are asked to take part as is reasonably profitable. The Far Eastern problem would interest the journalist, the diplomat, the economist, the political scientist, the philosopher, the businessman, and the representative of labor. Each one views the problem from a different angle and each one is prepared to demonstrate the reasons for a given conclusion after starting from an entirely different base. The magnitude of the subject

(104)

warrants the use of five or more speakers. The question is: How can five or more speakers on one subject be heard on the same program without a great deal of confusion and wrangling ?

Each panel speaker is advised before starting that the time for his main talk is limited. The usual allowance of time is ten minutes and no more. When the speaker knows that his time is severely limited he thinks of how he can make his arguments or present all his thoughts in the fewest possible words. Invariably the speakers on a panel present their own point of view and make reference to what has been said before. Only the first speaker does not have the advantage of what others have said before him, but all the rest do. It therefore does not take very long before areas of agreement begin to appear. Each succeeding speaker refers to his predecessor and indicates wherein they agree or disagree. It is not necessary to do so but it is a good idea. It helps to avoid repeating many things that have been said before. Theoretically each speaker is supposed to add to the greater fund of knowledge of the listeners.

In the handling of the panel discussion the chairman plays a very important part. He begins by making a short statement of fact about the topic of discussion. He limits himself to a maximum of five minutes. Upon completion of his introductory remarks he immediately gets the panel started. In the panel the chairman meets a very severe test. The participants are all individuals of some importance. All of them are entitled to the same consideration and respect, yet it is impossible to find five individuals who are all equal in their accomplishments and their right to be considered important in the eyes of their fellow men. To overstate one man's repu-

(105)

tation is to leave yourself open to a situation in which the really deserving one will have to be given a build-up that might sound fantastic. This is avoided by insisting that each speaker *give* a short biographical sketch that is to be used by the chairman as an introduction. Few men or women will make such a biographical sketch too long or boastful. We now assume that the matter of introduction is out of the way. We come to the problem of time.

You will recall that in Chapter 3 you were advised to demonstrate from the very outset that you as chairman are boss and that you intend to keep the time limit set. See to it that you do. When the ten-minute or whatever time limit that was previously set has been reached, you rise promptly and proceed to the point where the speaker is holding forth. If there is a separate table for the chairman or a separate desk, you tap for the speaker's attention and stop him. Make no excuses and no apologies. Go immediately into the business of introducing the next speaker. It is good to designate them by number before giving their names: thus, "The third speaker on the panel is a former}}, Mr. John Johns."

After all the panel speakers have been heard, they should be permitted to question one another. This type of questioning will help clarify some doubtful utterance and also will help enlarge the area of agreement. Of course it is possible that a panel discussion may enlarge areas of disagreement, but such is rarely the case in panel discussions.

Another problem in planning and chairing a panel discussion is the matter of obtaining the speakers. The answer to this problem is found in Chapter 2 ("How To Get Your Man"). If the suggestions contained therein are followed, there can be no doubt about success.

(106)

THE CONFERENCE

The conference form of meeting is nothing more nor less than a series of organized panel discussions with an additional twist. The panel discussion, it will be recalled, is a self-contained proposition which starts and finishes with the panel activities as a unit. The conference is the result of the combined panels. All of us have read about or attended conferences. (If you haven't, you should. There is always something or someone worthwhile.)

In the conference a group of panels are chosen with the same idea in mind as the single panel discussion—that is, the group thoroughly analyzes a part of a larger subject and then proceeds to draw such conclusions from the opinions expressed as would be of interest and value to others attending the conference. It works something like this.

A one- or two-day or even week-long conference is held. Before convening, a number of individuals are notified in advance that they are to take part with others in discussions involving given phases of a subject. Members of the same panel try as far as possible to arrange with each other exactly what it is each one will stress. Each panel has a panel chairman or convener. Notes are kept of what is said and what appears to be the field of agreement and disagreement. After a given time all of the panel chairmen come before the entire assemblage and make reports. These reports are supposed to be a transmission of the composite ideas of all the panels. As a general rule the reports of the panel chairmen are recorded verbatim and these reports are made into a conference report, to be distributed to all interested groups and individuals. Frequently, these reports are put on file in libraries, universities, museums, and other places of learning.

Conferences are held at regular intervals by organizations

that function on the basis of exchange of ideas. National and state-wide organizations most frequently hold conferences in the manner described above. There are from time to time international conferences. Their method of functioning resembles very closely that of the national and state groups.

Church groups are always meeting in conferences all over the world. Here in America we have, besides religious and church groups, such organizations as the League of Women Voters, the League for Industrial Democracy, the American Medical Association, the American Manufacturers Association, and a host of others. All of these meet from time to time to swap ideas for the benefit of all their members and any others who may be interested.

The scope of the conference is generally an all-embracing one, so that a conference by the League of Women Voters might be expected to try finding the answers to the perplexing question, "America's Role in the Fight for Democracy." Only a moment is necessary to appreciate how vast this field is. The League for Industrial Democracy would unhesitatingly tackle the problem, "The World in the Second Half of the Twentieth Century and Afterwards." A review of conference topics in the past will prove instructive.

One of the best features of the conference is the opportunity afforded everyone to take part in either a small or large way. At the time of a panel discussion there is very often a question and discussion period. For the members who like to serve on committees there are a thousand and one details to be attended to. Everyone can help or take part in the swapping of ideas. Conferences are demonstrations of democracy in action. The more there are, the better for all the world.

Chapter 8

PLANNING AND RUNNING A TRADE UNION MEETING

THE TRADE-UNION field is a most interesting and exciting one. It is different from almost any other because each union's purpose is almost always the same in every instance, yet the problems to be faced require different attacks each time. Men and women organize into a union because they all have the same ideal in mind; that is, they combine their activities for common economic advantage in the form of better wages and better working conditions generally. Members of a trade union are all part of a particular field of work. They have many things in common. They all must labor for their livelihood. Their problems are the same because they all work at the same trade—all steel workers are interested in steel, all automobile workers are interested in the automotive industry, etc. With all this, however, they still have an intense interest in the welfare of each other.

It may be surprising to many people to know that there are millions of working men and women in America and elsewhere who are not yet organized into trade unions. Each day new unions are being organized or started on the road to organization. The number of methods used to organize a trade union are many. Each method has been tried fully but not always successfully. From all the successes and failures some basic ideas have evolved. Let's look and see how to use them. It all adds up to meetings, meetings, meetings.

Suppose that we are going to try to organize a meeting in the textile industry with the idea in mind that from the meeting we will form a union of men and women who work in a given factory. It is the meeting we are concerned with here. We must begin by studying a number of things first. The following is a sample outline:

(1)   Study the company.

a)   Does the company operate a single plant, or is it a division of a larger outfit?

b)   Is the plant one that specializes in a particular branch of industry?

c)   What is the pay rate of the plant in comparison with that of others? What is the comparison of this plant with others as far as other working conditions are concerned, such as hours, shift-pay differentials, bonuses, vacations, etc.

d)   What is the make-up of the people employed? Are the workers of different nationalities, races, religious beliefs?

e)   What sort of facilities are available for holding meetings ?

f)   Check on all local facilities that can be used to advantage.

g)   Are there union meeting halls nearby ?

h) Can a local minister or priest or rabbi or some prominent person in the area be induced to take part in an organization meeting?

Keep in mind that this is not a union membership meeting. It is a meeting to start a union going.

(2)   After you have checked all of the things listed above, you are ready to work toward that successful get together.

In almost every instance the local newspapers will not carry any spot announcements. The radio stations will not do so either. Therefore you must depend upon a direct appeal method, i.e., by going directly to the individuals you are anxious to attract. If possible you see 10 or 15 of those you judge most likely to show some interest and invite them to an informal pow-wow. You invite them to come to a place that is familiar and acceptable to them. Ask them to name the place. Never mind what *you* think. What *they* think is important. If the prospective members prefer a lunchroom or a church basement or a side room in a social club, you go to the place of their choice.

In this first meeting with the small group, you do nothing more than convince them that a big meeting of all the workers in the plant should be held to hear what it is all about. You highlight your best proposition and try to get the members of the smaller group to feel that it is their idea. In doing things in this manner, you have that which is so necessary for every successful meeting. You get each member of the group to look upon the meeting as his or her own. Right then and there, try to get each one of the group to take on a special job. You must be ready, willing, and able at all times to help anyone who may need it. From this small group you manage to get the chairman of the coming big meeting. Ask the advice and assistance of the group to get just the right man or woman. All the meeting plans are developed by you in a subtle manner. By dropping a hint here and there, you succeed in getting from the persons present exactly what it is you are looking for.

(3) When all details such as time, place, publicity, and —if possible—a local person as one of the speakers have been settled, you let the matter rest, and you begin concentrating on the person who is to be the chairman of the coming

(111)

meeting. The way he cooperates at the coming meeting is going to determine whether you get the people behind you or not. You are about to be faced with a situation that is different from all other situations. In other parts of the book we have said again and again, "When you are the chairman, don't do too much talking. Say your piece in two or three minutes and then stop." This is going to be an exception to the rule.

The chairman of this meeting is a member of the local community. That does not necessarily mean he must actually live in the community. He is a part of the community because he works with the people you are anxious to have at the meeting; or he may be popular with the people you are trying to attract. This chairman calls the meeting to order. He is the fellow who is the center of attraction. You have carefully prepared him (or her) for the work. In the time that elapses between the meeting of the small group and the big meeting, you must arrange to meet the chairman a number of times. First you explain in broad terms the need for a free and open meeting to which all of the employees are invited, and then, as you get to know him better, you explain some of the finer points. He is going to be the person who sets the "tone" of the meeting. You suggest to him the important things to stress. As a trained person you know what is important to your union. You have been taught what to play up to new union members and you in turn tell it to the chairman. Besides this, you arrange with him the speakers' list. If possible, have him pick one or two of the group to get up and say something about the purpose of the meeting. You are *not* to be the first or second speaker. The meeting must be "pepped up"; the curiosity of the crowd should be whipped up. There's a stranger in their midst and they want to see and hear him. What sort of a fellow is he? How does he speak? What's his game? Bear all these things in mind when you plan the meeting with the chosen chairman. If he is untrained you must take the time to show him how to stand and how to sit. Rehearse with him the opening sentences. The more time you spend, the surer you are that the meeting will be a success.

What else do you do to promote the coming meeting? There are so many, many things that can and must be done that we can only discuss here a few of them. For example, you *give* out leaflets at the factory gate—short, well-worded leaflets, the kind of stuff you can read in a few seconds. The printing should be in large type. All names, dates, and places must be very clear and outstanding. If you are writing about wages in the plant, you write, "Do you know that the rate of pay in plant X is $1.50 per hour for job so and so? In this plant the rate is $1.30. Are you second-grade workers, or do you think you are entitled to the same pay as the workers in plant X. Come to the meeting at Tinbones Hall on Tuesday, October 10 at 6:45 P.M. sharp. There you will get all the facts from people who know. Remember the time, place, and date."

Before the time of actual meeting you must arrange for the workers to receive cards when they come into the hall. On these cards they can write their names, addresses, and any other important information you need. At the entrance to the hall is literature. Free literature. No charge for anything.

As many people from the community as you possibly can get are given jobs to do to help make the meeting a success. Remember that they like to be looked upon as persons of importance doing an important job.

Check details such as the flag on the platform, a table for speakers, live microphones, the number of chairs on the

(113)

platform, the people who are to be seated on the platform, etc.

Now the meeting itself: Try to start and finish the whole thing in a little less than two hours. Be prepared to patch up the bad work of poor speakers. Unless a miracle happens, you will have speakers who do say the wrong thing or say the right thing the wrong way. Someone was not invited to sit on the platform who should have been. Watch for these things. You must take care of putting all things right. Questions will be asked that the chairman cannot answer. Arrange with the chairman to call on you whenever that occurs. Don't shove yourself in there and show up the chairman as an amateur. Give him a chance to answer the questions. Keep in mind that you are looking to win favor in the eyes of the strangers—very frequently, distrustful strangers. If the chairman makes a mistake, ask him if you can help out with the questions. Don't tell him he's wrong. Remember: you want to help out. It goes against the grain less when you appear to be helpful and not bossy or too "smart."

You are the principal speaker. It is your turn at about the halfway mark. This is the kind of meeting at which you are prepared to speak for 30 or 40 minutes. No more. This is the kind of meeting where facts count. Oratory is good if you tie it in with facts. Stories are good to tell if they drive home the facts. Always remember that facts, facts, facts are the things that count.

In every meeting you will find a "wise guy" or "smart aleck." Handle him very calmly. Kill him with kindness. Be very, very patient. If you are calm and collected you can always get the "wise guy" to make a nuisance of himself. If you attack him you make a martyr of him and he becomes a champion of his fellow-workers. Warn the chairman about this sort of thing. Have the chairman work you into the position of tackling the "wise guy" and the doubting Thomases.

By all means have a question period, but not a question period that goes on and on and on. A short, active question period is effective. At the proper moment the meeting should be adjourned, but only after announcing that there will be other meetings. Where the chairman is new and untrained put in writing all announcements. Adjourn when the meeting is in a high mood. Cut it short and sharp. Don't let it drag. Your meeting has been a success.

There's a difference between running a meeting of a trade union or a fraternal organization and a meeting of citizens who gather together for one particular occasion.

The chairman of a union meeting is always a member of the organization. He was chosen for the job because the other members of the organization felt that he was the one who could do a good job. His obligations are different from those of most other chairmen because there are set methods of conducting a meeting in almost every union.

It is an unfortunate fact that even though most unions do have a prescribed method of opening and running their meetings, the chairmen frequently spoil things because they don't know how to go from one step to the other. Not only is that so, but many men and women who occupy the chair in a trade union or fraternal organization do not even know the proper way to address the members or how the chair is to be addressed.

One rule to remember is that in all trade unions and fraternal organizations you address the chairman as either "Brother Chairman" or "Comrade Chairman" or "Friend Chairman." Never in such organizations address the chairman as "Mr. Chairman" or "Madam Chairman." If the person in the chair is a female, you address the chairlady as

(115)

"Sister Chairlady" or "Comrade Chairlady," if the term "comrade" is used.

In some fraternal organizations the term used is different than in any other organization. In that case you must always use the term designated by the organization.

In the union meeting, the chairman has an advantage because the persons in attendance do not have to be approached in the same manner as the citizens who are gathered together for a protest meeting because the garbage doesn't give off the scent of roses after being one week on the street.

The trade-union meeting is called for a purpose that always has direct relationship to the broad purposes for which the union was established. The audience is always composed of the union members. Only when a mass meeting is being held by a trade union or fraternal organization to take up the cudgels for some general matter does the chairman's job change a bit. He then can proceed as described in Chapter 5.

Chapter 9

THE INFORMAL ROUNDTABLE DISCUSSION
AND GROUP PARTICIPATION

THE MOST enjoyable type of meeting is the round-table one. The term "round-table discussion" does not mean that there is a round table or for that matter there need not even be a table. The term originated from the expression sitting "around the table discussing." We still do sit around the table and discuss matters of interest in homes where exchange of ideas is substituted for television séances.

On every hand one hears loud lamentations that the home is no longer a place where ideas are exchanged. Enjoyable conversation is supposed to be a fast-disappearing art. If this is so, then the world is certainly the loser. Nothing can substitute for the "round-table discussion" or its cousin the college "bull session." This then is what we are talking about. Everyone is at ease and there is a complete absence of tension. Here the best thinking is done by the speaker and the listener. The invisible barrier that exists between the formal lecturer and his audience is completely gone. This is so to such an extent that it even affects the manner of dress of both the speaker and audience. Each one is on his own. The speaker may sit or stand or rest one foot on the chair in front of him or perch precariously on the edge of the table. Virtually everything goes. The members of the audience can sit with their chairs tilted backward or the back of

(117)

the chair being used as an arm rest. All pretense at formalism is brushed aside. This type of meeting is generally held in a home, a club room, or small meeting hall, or possibly in a lounge at the university. (A fine example of a university lounge is the one used by the women at the N.Y.U. Washington Square Division. It is beautifully appointed and lends itself to the easy exchange of ideas.)

The speaker and the questioners use the conversational tone. It is not necessary to rise to ask a question or take part in the discussion. Here more than anywhere else the timid souls, the introverts, the unsure get a chance to be heard. The entire surroundings are warm and friendly with no stuffiness or restraint.

Sometimes a home can be the scene of an informal dis-cussion-group gathering. In this case the home must be a comfortable one and those present must not be packed in so closely that they feel like intruders. When a home is chosen it must meet all of the requirements of the informal discussion group. The home meeting place must immediately *give* to a stranger the feeling that here he is welcome—the kind of welcome that invites you to stretch out comfortably on the floor near the antique china closet and still afford a good view of the speaker. While each guest is expected to be careful about the furnishings in the home, there must not be that fear of moving about freely. Only in an exceptional case can one find a free and easy atmosphere in the home where the guest is greeted at the door by a stiff-spined flunky or a housekeeper who appears to be annoyed by the appearance of "outsiders." It is better to limit the number invited and give those who come something to remember rather than to make it "a more the merrier" gathering. Bear in mind that every meeting has a purpose and it is always the hope of the sponsors of the meeting that the meeting will put the purpose across.

What is one of the chief purposes of the informal discussion group? To get everyone in the group to take part. Instead of sitting about and listening to the speaker hold forth, he really becomes a discussion leader. His remarks are aimed primarily at starting the group thinking for themselves about the subject of the evening. When his talk-in-chief is over, he subtly gets the audience to take over and proceed along lines that he lays out in an imperceptible manner. There is cross-questioning among the audience and, if the speaker has been stimulating, more heated discussion. The chairman steps in only for a moment from time to time to keep a semblance of order. Not too much interference— just enough to get everyone back on the right track again and maybe to *give* the speaker another chance to utter a few more sentences.

The preliminary plans for the informal meeting do not require as much intensive work or even the same kind of work as the large formal meeting. Since the number at the informal meeting will be small, we need concentrate only on a brisk telephone and word-of-mouth campaign. It will not be too much effort to add a few handwritten invitations to some special people. Don't worry too much if the local blurb sheet doesn't give your notice a full-column spread. If they so much as mention your meeting in one or two lines you've done a good publicity job. You pass over the lack of big notices in the newspapers.

The mistaken impression has gotten around that every meeting of every type, size, or nature should be written up in the newspaper, otherwise the meeting has been a failure from the point of view of "publicity." This is not so at all.

(119)

Realize that thousands of items reach each newspaper each day. The editors must select that which is most likely to attract wide attention. Is it reasonable to expect that an informal talk by Professor Proof at the home of Mrs. Thaddeus Smith, Jr. is going to get as much notice from readers as an after-dinner speech by the governor of the state? Oh no. This may be changed around if Professor Albert Einstein were to *give* an informal talk at any time anywhere. There is only one Professor Einstein and everything he says or does is news and it must be important (who are we to say otherwise?).

Small meetings are the kind that will get ideas across to people who come together because those who come are usually very much interested in the subject at hand. Big meetings lack this atmosphere. The large meeting is an impersonal affair. The air is full of formality—none of this easy *give* and take. In the large meeting we go to be talked at, in the informal meeting we stand a better chance to talk to and talk at.

How do we handle the round-table discussion group ?. We pick a committee that is able to function as a *unit* with a *minimum* show of effort. Each arriving guest is greeted by name or by a *warm,* "Good evening. We're glad you came. I am Rebecca-of-the-Wells. May I help you with your wraps?" or "Good evening, Mrs. Samson. Your neighbor, Mrs. Delilah, is here. She is sitting over there. It's nice to have you with us." A *smile* or a nod and here and there a handshake. All of them make up part of the stock in trade used by the welcoming committee.

As the guests arrive, some *two* or *three* members circulate about and offer tea or coffee or cool drinks—some cookies, too, if the organization can afford it. Napkins *al-*

(120)

ways, please. Choose committee members who can move about like slithering eels. *Keep the jungle pounders out of the way.* They can be placed around the room to hide the cracks in the plaster or maybe stimulate the flow of conversation among the guests.

The meeting has been called for 8:30 P. M. The chairman has been busy getting ready for the start. What has he been doing? The same thing the chairman did for the meeting in Chapter 3. Remember? For a failure to remember the chairman sometimes pays a big price. Take this little fiasco, for example: A very large meeting was being held one day in a nearby city. The committee in charge had done a magnificent job. Everything was working perfectly. The newspaper publicity was more than they ever hoped for. Every telephone call brought an assurance of attendance. Letters were answered promptly and a goodly number of leading citizens were honorary members of the committee to greet the guest speaker. The chairman was all primed for his job except that he failed to make certain that he remembered the name of the speaker. He started well and went along well and then wound up with a flourish as follows: "And now, ladies and gentlemen, I have the distinct honor and pleasure to introduce to you the speaker of the evening Mr. Lowell Thomas, the leader of the Socialist Party of the U. S. A." The laughter almost drowned out the applause. The chairman was stunned for a moment—he didn't realize what had happened until a much embarrassed member hastened to remind him that the speaker's full name was Norman Thomas. The balance of the evening went off well but the obvious discomfort of the chairman gave many people in the audience a slightly unhappy feeling. Mr. Thomas carried the humorous situation along and opened by assuring the chairman and the audience that while he did not at all share

(121)

Lowell Thomas' political views, he would enjoy sharing an opportunity to earn Lowell Thomas' income. (For the benefit of the non-listening radio fans, Lowell Thomas is a well-known newscaster of the more conservative school.)

A story similar to the one about Norman Thomas is told about Professor Coleman B. Cheney. He is a professor of economics at Skidmore College. He had been invited to address a group of students at a summer seminar session. To appreciate the story better a description of Professor Cheney should be included. He is a man of slight build, wiry and rather devoid of hair except for a modest crown. The first impression of the professor is that of a well-bred scholarly gentleman with a twinkle in his eye. In height he is about 5'4". There you have our man. The student chairman was waxing eloquent about Professor Cheney. He knew his entire pedigree and made good use of this information; and then came the thunderclap: "... and now it gives me pleasure to introduce to you Professor of Economics at Skidmore College Lon Chaney." In a jiffy the students pounced on this faux pas, and one was heard to call out: "He doesn't look like the phantom of the opera to me." Another wit caught on and shouted: "Aw, he's been dead so long he's shrunken. That's only the ghost." There are hundreds, maybe thousands of stories of this kind that can demonstrate how unfortunate it is for a chairman to fail to remember the full and correct name of a speaker. He must make sure of the speaker's name, his pedigree, his special claims to fame that the speaker wants mentioned, etc. The chairman and the speaker in a casual manner discuss the length of time the speaker will take for his main talk, the length of time to be consumed by the question period, followed by a discussion period, and finally an opportunity for the speaker to sum up. If there is more than one speaker, the chairman, in addition

(122)

to the above, also arranges the *order of speaking* and possible cross-questioning of one another by the speakers. If all the speakers are in agreement in their approach to the subject there is no sense in permitting the speakers to question each other. If there are differences among the panel speakers, permit cross-questioning—also comments on the answers given by members of the panel. That is, one speaker may comment on the answers of another. It adds a great deal of zest to the meeting.

Whenever there is a panel of speakers you may rest assured that a good time will be had by all provided the speakers are not stuffed shirts and they really have differences of opinion.

At first all questions are directed to the speakers and then all speakers are allowed to take part in answering questions. Soon the speakers start taking exception to the answer made by one of their number. The challenging speaker insists that his is the correct answer and not the other. His assertion is challenged in turn and then the speakers begin firing questions at one another. The discussion grows hot and very exciting. The chairman tries as long as possible to avoid stepping in. But the moment that things either *get* bogged down or seem to be getting out of hand, the chairman takes over and starts the proceedings all over again. More questions, more answers. More challenges and counter-challenges. Questions from one speaker to another followed by answers that are almost always unacceptable to the questioner.

About 20-30 minutes is enough for this sort of indoor sport. As a final gesture the chairman takes over, asks the speakers to wind up, and then closes the meeting with thanks all around.

Everything is done in advance. Unlike the large gathering,

(123)

it is all right to start our informal meeting a few minutes after the designated hour—say four or five minutes. There have been instances where the audience has been known to arrive ahead of time in such large numbers that the meeting could be started before the designated hour. This happens when the speaker or speakers are "big name" persons or where the meeting concerns a matter about which there has been much discussion and great excitement. Should the meeting be opened before the hour set ? No. Quick thinking is what is needed. Someone gets up to open the meeting for some preliminary business. What is preliminary business? (1) Announcements such as events to come and the personalities involved; the present drive for membership that is being conducted by the organization; the need for volunteer help. (2) A brief word or two about the purpose of the organization, how it functions, where it meets, its purposes, how one may join, and the advantages of joining. (3) Calling attention to literature left on the seats, available at the door, or being given out by the ushers.

When preliminary business is being handled, be sure that it ends at exactly the time the meeting is supposed to begin. The person in charge of the preliminary business ends by saying: "And now I'll turn the chair over to the chairman of the evening, Mr. Topper." When the chairman is ready to start he should signal to committee members to cease being busy.

In well-organized meetings a group of committee members is always about, attending to the inevitable last-minute details. Some are ushering, others are greeting arrivals whom they invited or who are regular attendants. One or two or more may be giving out interest cards or literature or membership blanks or what not. When the chairman is actually ready his pre-arranged signal should cause all activity by committee members to stop, except of course the ushering of latecomers to their seats. He invites the speaker or speakers to sit with him at the table where he is going to preside. He remains seated and comments on the fact that he is remaining seated, as for example: "Good evening, ladies and gentlemen (or "Good evening, folks," if you prefer)."—Bear in mind that these are not the only or even preferred types of greetings. It is safe to say that as many as fifty forms of greetings may be used and all with good effect. The greetings quoted here are the simplest that come to mind and are most often heard.—"Since our meeting this evening is to be an informal one I trust you will permit your chairman to remain seated so that he may feel himself one of the group."

The chairman must not continue along this vein trying or hoping to get an answer. It is taken for granted that the audience has no objections and furthermore they like the idea of,the chairman's being part of the whole group. He has done all he need do by way of getting consent to remain seated. Now we go on: "On behalf of the Society of Blushing Sunflowers, I welcome all of you. This evening we are to hear from a distinguished authority the story of the origin of red-headed Zulus. You may recall that about a month ago a number of dispatches . . ." (For about one minute you very, very *briefly* outline the subject.) "To know therefore a great deal more about this fascinating subject, we have asked Professor Bore to *give* us the pleasure of hearing him discuss 'Red—what is it and why'."

The speaker takes over and the chairman *somehow* becomes inconspicuous. When we say "somehow becomes inconspicuous" we do not mean that he disappears or crawls into a hole. The chairman moves out of the limelight by moving away from the speaker. A foot or two away is suffi-

(125)

cient to accomplish the job. When a chairman wants all eyes on the speaker and not on himself he can achieve this very easily. In an inconspicuous manner he finds a place just far enough away to make it seem that he too is a part of the listening audience. He gives this impression to the rest of the audience by looking directly at the speaker and paying strict attention to him. When the chairman is doing this the other members of the audience will do likewise. Observe a chairman concentrating his attention on the speaker and you will invariably find the audience doing likewise.

On the table before the speaker is water in a clean, sparkling pitcher, some paper cups or shining glasses, an ash tray, matches, a pencil, and a scratch pad. (Smoking is permitted.) The chairman may smoke but not like the chimney of a Pittsburgh steel plant. In the large formal meetings *it* is not right or proper for a chairman to smoke. As explained before, the chairman by his actions and attitudes greatly influences the audience before him. This taboo on smoking does not apply to the chairman of the small informal meeting. It is permissible for the chairman to smoke, but in doing so he should indulge in this form of pleasure without attracting attention. If, for example, the chairman is a pipe smoker he should be careful to do and to avoid doing certain things, (1) A chairman should avoid cleaning his pipe in preparation for reloading. (2) He should avoid making frantic efforts to locate his elusive pipe, tobacco pouch, matches, lighter, or the occasional pipe cleaner. (3) He should puff on his pipe lightly and emit the smoke in such a manner that he does not look like a New York City Fire Department smoke ejector. The pipe smoker who draws his cheeks in with gusto as his jawbones stand out in terrifying relief and then proceeds to blow rings from rounded puckered lips formed in the cherubic jowls is a perfect nuisance at a meeting. The chairman who does this is guilty of a crime and should be punished. Don't do it. (4) He should load his pipe before he starts the meeting and have it ready for lighting or relighting. He should not load his pipe and start tamping the tobacco into the bowl as the speaker tries to hold the attention of the audience. (5) He should not attempt to light his pipe if it's one of those that misses and resists all efforts to make it work.

If the chairman is a cigar smoker he should: (a) Avoid unwrapping his cigar from a cellophane wrapper or container, (b) Avoid playing absent-mindedly with the glittering cigar band, (c) Avoid biting fiercely at the end of the cigar as though he's a jungle animal tearing a limb from its stubborn socket. (Did you ever notice the cigar smoker who bites the rear end off and then puffs the front end before lighting up? He's probably blowing the dust out of the tobacco-leaf crevices.) He should *not:* (a) take good healthy draws followed by volcano-like eruptions; (b) chew the end of the cigar as though *it* were a bazaar-sized package of double-bubble gum.

The cigar smoker, like the pipe smoker, should always bear in mind that the overwhelming majority of people cannot smell the odor of cigar or pipe smoke without feeling ill. Try to keep away from the persons near you at the meeting.

We come now to the cigarette smoker and his sins of omission and commission. The chairman should follow the following rules:

(1) Don't start opening a new package of *cigarettes* with the accompanying symphony of cellophane-crackling sounds.

(2) Don't start tapping the top of the package in order to force out one of the reluctant "butts."

(127)

(3) Don't try lighting the cigarette with a lighter that never seems to work in a crisis. Use a match and be done with it.

(4) Avoid "frisking" yourself to snare that misplaced package of cigarettes.

(5) When stamping out a lighted cigarette, don't pound it as if you wished to pulverize it. A well-aimed careful stroke and the lighted head of fire is knocked off. A doubling over of the remainder of the cigarette and it's all over.

(6) Never offer cigarettes all around as though inviting a campaign of smoke against the speaker.

The best rule of all is not to smoke at all. If you must, then do so by having the pipe clean and filled; the cigar should be trimmed and prepared in advance; the package of cigarettes should be open and the cigarettes loosened; and in all cases keep the amount of smoke down to a minimum.

Why is so much said about smoking? Because we have here an example of one of the many things a chairman must be cognizant of in order to avoid distracting the audience. Every move is seen and every move causes a reaction in some or all of the listeners. The reaction of the listeners should be to the speaker's words and gestures, and not to anyone else's. Smoking is used to illustrate the point because it lends itself so well.

The chairman may make notes but not with wide flourishes. A chairman is within his rights when he makes notes of a the speaker's utterances either in preparation of questions or for information. When done by a thoughtful chairman, taking notes aids the speaker. The members of the audience who observe the chairman doing this feel that it must be important and they are even more attentive. The thing we want to warn against is the alert chairman who forgets himself and suddenly goes into action, furiously writing to note carefully something the speaker has just said. It is obvious from the look on the chairman's face and the manner in which he begins scribbling that he does not agree with the speaker. Immediately the audience is distracted. What is it the speaker said that: sent the chairman off that way? The listeners begin thinking back and soon they do not hear what is being said. After a few moments they are back trying to catch up on what the speaker said during the few seconds they were trying to discover what sent the chairman off. Confusion is added to confusion. That is why a chairman should learn to make notes in an almost imperceptible manner. Use the manner of one who is genuinely interested. Whether it involves taking notes or just being a part of the audience, always develop the art of looking and acting intensely interested in the talk. This fact cannot be stressed too strongly. It does not take much training, but it does do much good. If the speaker continues beyond the allotted time, he should be permitted to go on for a reasonable additional period, and then a note should be put in front of him reminding him that the time is up. If there is a panel of speakers, no extension of time is granted. *Call time when it is up.* Too often a chairman is reluctant to cut a speaker off. This must be avoided. A precise time limit keeps the meeting in good shape. It avoids the air of slovenliness. When the time is up and the speaker is halted by the chairman, the interest of the audience is heightened because: (a) a firm chairman is appreciated by all thinking and orderly-minded people, and (b) proponents and opponents have something to focus their emotional reactions on. Another thing to remember: when time is called at the right moment, the audience as well as the speaker gets the feeling that all thinking has to be done on an organized basis. None of this wandering all over the lot. There is so much time allotted and no more, so the ideas had better be lined up correctly and succinctly. Remember, then, that the only exception to the rule of strict adherence to time is the occasion of the single speaker.

There is one sin that a chairman commits only on rare occasions, but it is serious enough to warrant our taking notice of it. Every now and then a chairman finds a very close friend or even an incessant talker sitting next to him, across the aisle, or on the opposite side of the table. Sometimes the chairman but most often the other fellow starts a whispering campaign. It is only a word or two, but soon it is like a river—it goes on endlessly. The gabber talks behind the back of his hand, the chairman answers out of the side of his mouth. This is followed by semi-audible whispers addressed to the table top and a reply is made by the chairman in the sign language. All this is rude, inconsiderate, and distracting. The chairman must follow an iron-clad rule. No cross-comment at any time during the meeting with anyone, except at moments when all others are permitted to talk.

When the principal talk or talks have been delivered, the chairman takes over and begins the question and discussion period. Here the procedure is changed a bit. Something re-sembling the following transpires: The chairman rises and says, "Thank you, Professor Bore. Now all of us are that much better informed than we were earlier this evening. There will soon be a flood of questions. For those who may not know our procedure, we permit questions from all those present. Questions must be short and to the point. After each question Professor Bore will *give* an answer. At the end of half an hour we will have a discussion period. Let's have questions now."

Note the following: During the question period the chairman remains standing. This is done only when the questions

(130)

are short and the answers are short. It would be a bit silly to be popping up and down like a jack-in-the-box. Even though the chairman remains standing, he must learn how to keep out of the way. Where the questions require answers that take more than half a minute or so, the chairman should take his seat. If the speaker himself accepts the question from the audience, the chairman remains seated. He designates each person who is to be permitted to ask a question. During this time it is permissible for the committee members to move quietly about, serving tea or coffee or what have you. Note also that sometimes the speaker prefers that first all questions be asked and that he make his answers at one time. If the speaker prefers this procedure, it is right to do as the speaker asks. The second method described is preferable because in answering all of the questions at once the speaker goes into virtually another talk.

Whenever people are anxious to get across to others the ideas they have in mind, there is always one large and difficult problem, and that is: How can we get others to become enthusiastic about those things we believe in?

There is a growing realization on the part of those who work in the field of spreading ideas that mere lecturing or writing about these ideas is not the answer to the problem. Take, for example, the radio. This marvelous medium of communication of ideas is potentially so great that there is no adequate way of describing it, yet it has not revolutionized the way of life of the people of the world. Billions of words have been broadcast to the people of the earth by those good citizens who are anxious to do away with racial prejudice and discrimination. Thousands of talks have been given and almost all of them have been good. Has there been a very marked decrease in bigotry and discrimination and other attitudes of a like nature? No. Very definitely, no!

(131)

All this effort has helped a bit, of course, but not to a marked degree.

Volumes have been written by the score. In addition to books we have pamphlets, magazine article, and leaflets. Add to all this the motion pictures, the theater, and the preachings from pulpits and still we find the sad spectacle of blind unthinking hatred of man by man because the other fellow is black or yellow or brown or a Catholic or Jew or Protestant or a non-believer. There are sectional prejudices as well as a number of other kinds. These prejudices exist against ideas as well as against persons. The Fascist, the Nazi, the Communist all despise democracy as we know it. Their blind prejudice against democracy urges them on to commit acts of violence as well as less harmful acts.

How can these and similar problems be faced and successfully handled? It appears that the group-participation idea has so far proved the most successful of all methods tried. The procedure is simple and can be used by almost any organization.

Let us consider the proposition that it is possible to have a society consisting of persons absolutely free of all antagonisms. This is a most controversial subject and will immediately cause all sorts of reactions. Mrs. X is to be the discussion leader. This is not going to be a formal or even an organized informal talk. It is an arrangement in which the discussion leader starts out by making a broad general statement or by asking a question. The leader, of course, does have definite ideas on the subject but she does not want to force them on the group. Her intention is to have the group come to the same conclusion as her own. All right. She asks her question and then asks: Is there a main topic we must bear in mind when we discuss a matter of this kind ? A suggestion is made by one of the group. The discussion leader

(132)

writes it down and asks if all the others agree. If they do, the group goes on to develop the theme. New suggestions, new ideas are offered. During all this time the leader knows where she is going and what she wants the group to build up as its own. When the suggestions made are wrong or irrelevant or too vague, the leader subtly suggests what the right answer might be and gets one of the group to offer the idea as though it were something just discovered by these newborn thinkers. In a little while a large number of facts are developed. In short, quick sentences and phrases the whole idea starts taking shape, with a minimum of resistance to the new suggestions. Everyone is taking part. This is the sort of thing that gives the more timid members a chance to build up their ego. Participants learn to think and speak on their feet. They begin to learn how to respect the rights of others and to disagree. From their own group is evolved the conclusion that in reality the group leader was looking for. This method of meeting together makes for more informative and interesting get-togethers.

The group leader rarely if ever says, "No, that is wrong." The usual thing is, "Well, now let's see. Does anyone feel differently?" No one is offended or held up to ridicule. No feelings have been hurt; no resistance built up. The feeling of belonging takes hold and this feeling of belonging gives each individual a strong brace of security. Those who are secure are inclined to be happy—mentally and physically sound. Secure people do not need to brutalize others to feel safe in their place in the world. The participant in the group-discussion arrangement is secure even when his idea is not accepted, because he remains with the idea as it develops. If one of his suggestions is not accepted, another may be and so he has the feeling of contributing along with the others. The discussion leader is the equivalent of

(133)

the chairman and speaker combined. He or she must make every word count and must always be alert to the trend of thought of all the members of the group.

An added advantage of group participation is the keen desire to continue. The individual who has had a taste of taking part and has been exhilarated by his participation looks forward to the time when the group will meet again and he will have another opportunity to be in the limelight. Just as town meetings have become popular of late, group participation is bound to become more and more popular as another form of informal meeting.

To repeat: In an informal group gathering the chairman may not only smoke, just as everyone else does, but may address by name persons in the audience. The chairman may even from time to time make humorous comments about happenings at the meeting. DO NOT OVERDO THE BUSINESS OF MAKING HUMOROUS REMARKS DURING THE QUESTION PERIOD. (See comments on humor in Chapter 4.)

Follow the same procedure during the *discussion* period as was followed during the question period.

When the question and discussion periods are both ended, the chairman again thanks the speakers on behalf of the organization. He declares the meeting adjourned, but before doing so urges those present to remain for a continuation of the social hour. That's all there is. There is no more.

Chapter 10

BUSINESSMEN'S MEETINGS AND CONFERENCES

HARDLY a day goes by that does not have a meeting of businessmen going on somewhere in our country. This is a highly developed industrial country with a vast variety of industries scattered over the length and breadth of the land. There are never-ending problems that require businessmen to get together from time to time.

Long ago the representatives of business learned the value of getting together for the exchange of ideas. At first they would have nothing to do with each other. The business secrets of one firm were closely guarded so that competitors could be kept at a safe distance. Each firm was out to get all it could and the devil take the hindmost.

As the industrial revolution kept accelerating the rate of development and expansion of industry, some far-sighted capitalists began to realize that there are many, many problems common to all owners of plants and mines and mills and banks and public utilities. While it was true that they were competitors in business it was also true that they were part of a group that could benefit greatly by cooperation.

In the beginning it was chiefly the representatives of "big business" that met to discuss their problems. The meeting of small businessmen's groups is a development of the very recent past. It was the "big business" meetings and the things they accomplished that virtually forced small businessmen to get together for sheer survival.

How do meetings of big business or little business or both come about? Who calls them together and how? The question also arises, "Why do they meet?" All this we shall work out together in order to get at the correct answer.

With greater concentration of control over different branches of industry, the executives involved developed "institutes and conferences" and "committees." These names simply mean organized units of the same industry. When combined together they constitute chambers of commerce or manufacturers' associations or what have you.

Let us take a typical industry and see what happens.

We shall talk about the machine-manufacturing industry. There are literally hundreds of plants throughout the United States engaged in this type of work. They are members of a nation-wide association with national headquarters in one of our cities. One year ago the national organization met and at its annual meeting chose an executive board and officers for the year. These officers and executive board run the affairs of the organization between meetings. They are concerned with every conceivable problem that faces the industry. One of the problems is making all of the arrangements for the next meeting—the place has already been designated by the last convention. We will assume that the next meeting is to be held in the city of New York on April 1, 2, and 3. A group of members is chosen by either the president or the executive committee. This group is generally referred to as the committee on arrangements. They are called together by the secretary of the national organization for the purpose of organizing themselves into a functioning committee. They choose their own chairman and have a full-time paid secretary. (All secretaries should be on a full-time paid basis. The job of secretary is a difficult and endless one.) Once organized, they begin long in advance to plan all the details—and a large number of details they are. The following is a partial list of the committee's headaches—not in their order of importance.

(1) Circularizing members and gathering information about the number who are to attend.

(2) Setting up meeting headquarters:
  - a. which hotel to use
  - b. when shall headquarters be open
  - c. what service must headquarters be prepared to give

(3) Arranging for hotel reservations
  Contacting hotels in contracting for rooms
  Checking reservation with listings
  Arranging for luncheon
  Arranging for dinner
  Arranging for banquets
  Arranging for entertainment
  Arranging for tours
  Arranging for radio time
  Arranging for publicity

(4) Printing reports of:
  The President
  The Secretary
  Standing committees

(5) Arranging the speakers' list
  Public officials as speakers
  Specialists
  Outstanding industrialists and financiers
  Prominent scientists or engineers

(6) Committee rooms
  Panel discussions

(137)

Special committee conferences
Nominating committee

As was said before, this represents only a partist list of the details to be attended to—and the success or failure of the meeting may sometimes rest on the fact that one or two minor details go off on a tangent.

Why do businessmen meet when their time is so valuable and they are supposed to be so busy ? Well, the answer is simple once you figure it out. Business is the boiling cauldron of commercial and industrial life. Every day there are new ideas, new methods, new laws passed or proposed either in Congress or state and local legislative bodies, and, even more, there is the ever-present bogey of taxes and the endless fight against time. There are deals to be made with competitors and against competitors, political fence-building and house-cleaning and, of course, technical problems such as accounting, distribution methods, advertising, and reduction of overhead generally. Like an evil spirit the labor problem looms large and everywhere. Strange as it may seem, no businessman's conference ever winds up without admitting somewhere along the line that labor is not so bad after all. Be that as it may, the reasons why businessmen get together are many and complex. The usual thing of course is to have reports made by committees that were set up a year or two ago. For example: A committee may be appointed to investigate the possibility of standardizing internationally certain measurements or scales of measurement. This is a big job that requires the aid of a number of governmental departments, our diplomatic corps, and the representatives and even heads of foreign governments; it may require some treaty arrangements as well as uniform rules and regulations in a large number of countries. The accomplishment of such an aim may mean a drastic reduction in production costs.

The manufacturers are very much interested in knowing what was accomplished. All this information is given in the report of the committee that was appointed a long time ago.

The president of the organization calls the meeting to order. He presides at all sessions except when he calls upon one of the vice-presidents to take over the chair. The rules governing the actions, attitudes, and manners of the chairman as set forth in Chapter 14 apply here as well as they do in other meetings.

It would be unfortunate if the impression were given that all meetings of businessmen are as big and important as the one described above. There are meetings of business groups that resemble ordinary meetings. There is nothing very startling about them. Businessmen have a common purpose just like everyone else and therefore they get together at meetings. The business they transact is like the business of the local flower club or the Ladies Home for the Aged Auxiliary. The chairman calls the meeting to order. Reports of committees on special problems and projects are heard. A speaker who is a specialist in one phase of the business gives a talk and then there are questions and answers. On occasion there may be more than one speaker—but it all adds up to one thing: The attending members want information that will be of value to them. Businessmen's meetings almost always combine business with pleasure. For this they are to be commended. Too few people in our country think in terms of work and fun. The businessman knows that he can function best when he changes the routine of his everyday activity. Think of the vast difference between the reactions of the businessman's mind when he gets a chance to do something he likes and not worry about how well he does it and the pressure he feels as he goes through the process of carrying on a given project. That short period of time he spends knocking a ball around or thrilling to the joy of making a small or grand slam at bridge gives him a new pool of energy to draw on. In his meetings the idea is carried over and the combination of business and pleasure results.

The business groups don't have as much worry about attendance at meetings as the local flower club does, but they have their fair share. They are limited in the number to whom they can appeal. They suffer from much of the same indifference on the part of members as other groups do. On the other hand, they have the advantage of a concentrated number to work on. In addition, they have more money to work with than the average group has.

One last thing about businessmen's meetings. To meet the problems of the organization the active members must keep on devising ways and means of making every meeting an attractive one. This type of planning is found wherever meetings are held. What goes for one goes for all.

Chapter 11

THE MEETING THAT IS TO BE BROADCAST

FROM TIME to time you may be the chairman of a meeting that is to be the subject of a broadcast. It may be a banquet or a debate or a convention of one sort or another. The radio and television stations will be anxious to get your meeting on the air. It all depends on the amount of interest in the event. Be that as it may, you are planning for the hour of such a meeting. As an active member and as chairman, there are a number of things to keep in mind.

(1) The time for the broadcast or television is on the ex act moment previously set. If the station sets the hour at 8:30 P.M. it means *exactly* 8:30 P.M. and not 8:31 or 7:49 P.M. They work on split-second precision.

(2) To meet the exact time requires your stressing to all who are interested that the proceedings are to be broadcast; and you must repeat again and again the fact that everyone must be on hand *before* the time set in order to hear the introductions of the technicians who are going to do the broad casting.

(3) Acquaint yourself with all the things that must be said and done by you or anyone else involved. Write every thing down unless you are thoroughly familiar with the operation. If there is to be a sequence of actions write it down.

(4) Be prepared for any contingency and be ready to make last-second changes or substitutions. There are so many

possibilities of something going wrong that they are too numerous to mention, yet a careful organization of every detail will make the chances of success almost a certainty.

(5) If there is to be a broadcast that comes in the middle of the business of a meeting, be sure to arrange matters in such a manner that you can, without any effort or confusion, break in and switch from one thing to another.

(6) Always have on hand a committee that will be dispersed among the audience. This committee must be pre pared to go into action instantly. They may be called upon to whip up enthusiasm, help simulate certain sounds, urge the audience on to greater applause, or help keep them quiet —as the case may be.

When you are the chairman it may be your duty to introduce a speaker or speakers. Never depend on your memory even though you know the speaker for more than fifty years. Adlibbing on the radio is dangerous. *Write down every word of your introductory remarks.* Time your remarks and stick to them. Once the broadcast has begun you are only a sound-uttering human. The way you look or stand or pluck your ear is of no consequence. The microphone is taking care of the speaker and only he and it are involved. Keep out of the way and let science do its worst or best.

Everything is different, however, when the proceedings involve more than merely introducing a speaker. If you are the moderator and there is to be a question and answer period or a discussion period and different persons will be using the microphone from time to time, you as chairman are the most active persons of all. You indicate who is to speak and very frequently from which position. You may have to break in and tell a speaker to move up or signal him to move back. You may have to shut some speakers up or urge others to speak more loudly. If this is the situation you are in, then you must first acquaint yourself with the method of carrying out such functions. This is done by visiting studios or going to meetings where such activities are carried on. Much of the knowledge is in the chairman's own head. All you need do is figure out what the most logical thing is to do and then proceed. There is nothing mysterious about conducting a meeting that is being broadcast. Give it some thought and then check and see how close you come to being absolutely light.

What applies to radio broadcasting does not go for telecasting. In a telecast you are being observed and therefore you must adhere to the rules discussed elsewhere in this book.

The use of the microphone and all the equipment that goes with it has grown to be such a commonplace thing that no one gives it much thought. It is there and that is all there is to it.

Everyone knows that many times it would be impossible to hear what a speaker is saying if it were not for the public address system being used. Every chairman as well as every speaker ought to know how to use the microphone. Therefore, these few hints:

(1) Always remember that a microphone is part of a public address system. This system is used to amplify the sound of the voice. Amplification is done by the equipment. It is not accomplished by shouting or screaming. Let the instrument do its work—not your lungs and the voice box.

(2) When standing before a microphone there should be at least the distance from the extended finger tips to the el bow between the microphone and the speaker's mouth. Measure this distance and keep it at all times. Sometimes a speak er wishes to dramatize a statement by having the subdued or hushed tones emphasized. Speaking in a "spooky" manner helps drive a point home; the same is true about a very loud

(143)

assertion. To achieve both of these effects get close to the microphone and turn the head slightly to the side. When the very soft voice is used it is permissible to speak into the "mike" as well as to use a side approach.

(3) Avoid blocking the face with the microphone. It is extremely annoying for a member of the audience to keep looking in the direction of the speaker and find it impossible to see the full face. This causes a subconscious antagonism and irritation. In addition to all this, a very important part of the body becomes useless to the speaker. The face is used to help develop moods as well as emphasis. Humor is part face, part voice, and part personality. Face is the big factor.

For all of the reasons above, the "mike" should be adjusted so that it never comes higher than the bottom of the chin. If the "mike" is too high, lower it. Too low is just as bad as too high. A speaker should never be compelled to stoop over the microphone. It makes the speaker look ridiculous. The speaker or chairman who stops long enough to make the necessary adjustment of a microphone is impressive to the audience. Cultivate the habit when acting as a chairman.

In Chapter 4, we dealt with the general theme of humor. Radio and television, though both new fields, have given rise to a rich fund of anecdotes and humorous experiences. Just to give you a few samples, we are going to quote from Bill Leonard, the very capable commentator who broadcasts the "This Is New York" show for the Columbia Broadcasting System (WCBS). Mr. Leonard has kindly given us permission to reproduce the following remarks:

A broadcaster—particularly an interviewer—lives in constant fear of the guest whose gentle case of mike fright turns to sheer paralysis. It doesn't happen often, but when it does, all parties concerned, probably including the listeners, suffer tortures worse than a thousand commercial jingles.

My first, and worst, experience took place on Thanksgiving morning, 1946, when the guest on my "This Is New York" program was a local lady who had earned a solid reputation and a solider income designing table settings. After fitting and, as usual, overly flattering introductions, I asked her if she would describe her own Thanksgiving table.

She looked at me as if I had assigned her to shoot the President. Her jaw, underslung to begin with, rattled against the table edge. Glassy were her eyes. "Go ahead," I urged. "Tell us."

Her body twisted in agony. A racking sob battered against the microphone. "I can't! I can't! I can't!" she sobbed, in the best soap-opera tradition. She buried her head in her arms.

"Okay," I said. "Don't. How about some water. We're off the air now, take it easy." I went over to the cooler, got her a glass of water. She felt better.

"You know," she said brightly. "Isn't that the silliest thing?" We went on to discuss the problems of mike fright. In a minute or so she had launched into a description of her Thanksgiving table. Five minutes later the interview was over; she had performed like a trouper.

When I told her she had been on the air all the time, she fainted, again in the best soap-opera tradition, and I went to the water cooler again.

Another time I remember with affection was my fluff and mine alone. My guest on that particular morning was Joe E. Brown, who had just replaced Frank Fay in the perennial hit *Harvey*. "I'm proud to welcome to our show this morning," I began, "Joe E. Brown, currently starving in *Harvey.*"

There was, needless to say, a soaring silence.

Mr. Brown plunged into the breach.

"Ladies and gentlemen," he said, "I would just like to add to Mr. Leonard's able and accurate introduction that the government, not the management, is to blame."

Perhaps my fondest memory concerns an interview that never went on the air. When Dimitri Mitropoulos took the New York Philharmonic into the Roxy Theatre, I brought backstage a portable tape recorder for the inevitable transcribed chat. The Maestro was so fascinated by the recording machine, battery operated and smaller than a shoe box, that our fifteen-minute appointment stretched to an hour. "Where can I get one? How much does it cost ? Can I record music ? How soon can I get delivery?" He fired question after question. Finally we made our interview, complete with his delightful Greek accent. I thanked him, and he let me know he'd be listening next morning.

Back at the Studio, I found that not one word had recorded. Machines are human; this one had given up the ghost. Another guest—as it happened, then acting Mayor of New York City Impellitteri—replaced the Maestro on the broadcast the following day.

Later in the week I received the following note from Mr. Mitropoulos:

"Dear Mr. Leonard:

The machine is even more marvelous than you described. It not only made me Mayor of New York but removed my accent, too."

(146)

The next anecdote, told by Martha Deane, well-known and very popular commentator on Radio Station WOR, and reproduced with her kind permission, illustrates the human side of some so-called "important" people and the trouble which one slight slip of the tongue may cause:

When I was still a newspaperwoman, I had a great fondness and admiration for the late Mayor Fiorello La Guardia. Shortly after I came to WOR, I decided to ask Mayor La Guardia to be a guest on my program. He agreed to come at the very first opportunity. One day his secretary called and said the Mayor would be my guest on a given morning.

Everything went just fine. The Mayor arrived about fifteen minutes before broadcasting time. I began briefing the Mayor but he soon said: "Aw, come on, you know me and I know you. Let's get down to business." "Good," I said, "we'll do it just the way you like it."

After we had been on the air for about fifteen minutes, and the Mayor had done all the talking, I suddenly burst in with an apology for leave to do my commercial stint. Suddenly the Mayor interrupted and right over the air said to me: "Did I hear you say Minute Man Soup?" "Yes you did," I replied. "Well, folks, I can tell you all about this soup," said Mayor La Guardia, and for the next few minutes he told all our listeners about Minute Man Soup. He did a wonderful job.

Again we picked up the interview. More commercials and more interview. Suddenly I began to laugh out loud. My audience must have been bewildered, so I proceeded to explain as follows: "I can't help laughing. The Mayor is playing with my earrings." There was a moment of deadly silence and then the Mayor called out: "Be sure to tell the folks the earrings are not on you!"

The fact is that I had taken the earrings off and left them on the table. The Mayor had placed them on his own ears and was putting on a hilariously funny show with them. By his quick presence of mind he saved my career and his reputation.

Finally, as an example of the confusion which lack of knowledge of another person's native language can create, we quote the following incident as told us by that talented commentator Alma Dettinger of Radio Station WQXR:

A few years ago, when the great Italian tenor Ferruccio Tagliavini came to the United States, I was asked to interview him on "Other People's Business." With bravos for Tagliavini ringing in my ears and the WQXR musical bent in mind, I was delighted to do so. "Other People's Business" is almost invariably done without any written script, but I was assured that this guest would not appear without one. I waived the usual objections, so with the secretary, the star's press agent, etc., we set forth for Mr. T.'s apartment in New York.

Along the way I discovered that my interview guest spoke no English. I, of course, spoke no Italian. At the door, Tagliavini and translator greeted us cordially and from then on it was clear sailing. I asked the questions, the translator did his job, and Tagliavini gave the answers. Meanwhile the secretary took these down and later was to transcribe the interview into English phonetics which the star could read on the air. We parted with smiles and hand-kissing and friendly confidence.

The next morning, Mr. Tagliavini arrived late for pre-broadcast rehearsal. Upon seeing the script, I discovered that the secretary's phonetics and the singer's phonetics had gone to different schools together. However, Tagliavini sat down—five minutes before air time —in a brave attempt to rewrite the script in phonetics he could understand. We were on the air before you could say "WQXR" and into the interview with all consonants flying! It went rather too carefully for my taste so I decided to improve upon the studied delivery. Believing that my guest and I were *en rapport,* I felt sure I could make him understand me better than he understood the unfamiliar phonetics. Tossing aside my script, I began *to* question him along the lines of yesterday's prepared material.

"What are your usual hours of practice?" Tagliavini threw me a puzzled glance. "What do you think of the United States?" ... He shook his head sadly. Inspired, I hit upon the happy thought of dramatizing the question. Making very energetic and understandable motions of wielding the knife and fork, I asked a question he answered the day before. "Signor Tagliavini," I said slowly, with gestures, "what do you like to *eat* before singing . . . ?" A look of betrayal came into the singer's eyes. *"Eat,"* I repeated, raising the imaginary fork. His eyes went back to the script where in desperation he clutched at the first sentence that caught his eye. "What do you like to eat?" I repeated. "Oh," he replied carefully, "I like *Tosca . . .* and the *Barber of Seville."*

(149)

These few anecdotes, all of them arising out of real-life incidents, illustrate some of the thousand-and-one things that can happen in a radio interview or a meeting that is to be broadcast. Similar stories could be told by Bill Slater, Tex and Jinx, or any of the other outstanding performers on the air-waves and video screens at the present time.

Chapter 12

SPECIAL TYPES OF MEETINGS:
PRESIDING AT A FUNERAL

IT IS UNFORTUNATE, but once in a while we are called upon to take part in a funeral service for a departed friend. It is customary for friends and family to foregather to pay their respects to the departed. For the living and not for the dead, the custom has grown to have close friends utter the praises of the deceased just before the last walk earthward is begun. The occasion is always a sad one for someone and frequently a sad one for many. Time and again funeral services are conducted for an undeserving individual who managed to win the confidence of his gullible fellow beings. It means only a loss of some valuable time and a bit of soothing syrup for the family. If it does anyone any good no complaint should be made.

The occasion when a deserving one is on his way to the last resting place is the time when we especially want to know what to do and how to do it.

Assume that arrangements have already been made by the family for the funeral. The director knows the hour, the approximate number of persons expected to accompany the body, the name of the family members, etc. The Fraternal Order of High and Exalted Potentates, of which you are the Po of Potentates, has been requested to take charge of that part of the services in which the eulogies will be delivered.

You are the one who is assigned the task of organizing the array of elocutionary talent. Before the day in question you go to the home or funeral parlor. Pay your respects to the family of the deceased and then seek out the director. You and he get together and make arrangements for the hour at which the services are to begin. The director will tell you whether music is available and what provisions have been made for the religious services. If your organization has a set ritual, you follow that ritual; if not, proceed as though the departed belonged to no organized body. If the deceased was not a member of any organization, then try to arrange the procedure painlessly with a family member. If there is to be music, ascertain the type of music preferred. Some persons prefer instrumental to vocal and some would like both to be used. If hymns are to be sung, make note of the names of the hymns. For religious services jot down the name of the one who is to utter the prayer and finally ask if there are any particular persons the family would like to have called up to deliver eulogies. Check carefully on their names, relationship to the deceased, and the position of each speaker in the community. Remember this is a funeral and not a flower show. No puffing and no huffing.

On the day of burial you arrive about one hour before the services are to start. Check carefully every detail. Round up the speakers, the musicians, the preacher, and anyone else who is to take part. You tell each one exactly how you are going to proceed. There is no discussion, no debate. You yield to an intelligent suggestion; otherwise go right ahead with your plans. The service is to last a given length of time. From half an hour to an hour is usual. At the appointed time you take your place either on the podium or in front of the coffin and stand there silently for a few moments. Your presence there will bring quiet. Keep your voice soft and

(152)

subdued. Without any preliminaries you announce: "The invocation will be delivered by_____of_____." You re fer to his rank and his church or synagogue or mosque. When the prayer is ended you step back in position from which you originally started. Again no preliminaries. You start: "Friends, we are gathered here today to pay our last respects to Ephraim Swansong, our dearly beloved ..." You go on in this vein for five to ten minutes. Use the most flow ery and touching language at your command. Soft and easy is your manner of delivery. You refer to the flattering and commendable facts about the dead. You end. Pause and then proceed with the next item on the program. "The organist will play ..." The music ends. You introduce a speaker. In doing so, tell a bit about the speaker. Choose his most important bid for fame. No bowing to speakers. You step aside or take your seat. No applause ever at a funeral. Each time the same procedure is followed until all the speakers have finished. You call again upon the religious representative for the closing prayer. At the end thereof the director takes over and the job you set out to do is complete. Precision, sureness, dignity, and orderliness are absolutely required.

Chapter 13

GETTING RID OF YOUR NERVOUSNESS

WHENEVER the subject of a meeting comes up for discussion, the question of nervousness comes up at the same time. How often have we heard people say, "I couldn't be a speaker or a chairman if I had to save my life. I become so nervous whenever I try to speak that I forget everything I had in mind and I feel like a perfect fool." Sometimes we hear people say, "If I had to get up on my feet and speak or open a meeting, I would very likely drop dead at the first moment." There are a number of other things that people have said and still say about their nervousness in connection with meetings.

No one is ever completely free of some degree of nervousness on every occasion. Sometimes an old and seasoned speaker may find that he has no nervousness at all for a long period of time, and then, suddenly, a particular meeting begins to bother him, and before he knows it he too discovers his knees knocking inside those baggy trousers of his. A little nervousness is nothing to worry about. It is quite natural and can even be helpful. It sharpens your thinking and drives out thoughts of everything else except that which relates to the meeting.

We are going to suppose that you are to be the chairman of the evening or a speaker. Now we have before us the problem of how to overcome our nervousness. The devices

(154)

to be described are easy to use and have been found helpful by all those who have tried them.

Let us suppose that there is a lectern standing in the middle of the platform and you are going to speak from that spot. All your efforts to control your nervousness have been of no avail. The time has come to open the meeting or to start speaking. There can be no further delay. Walk up to the lectern and see where there are sharp points. Place the heel of your thumb against the sharpest point visible and proceed to press against such sharp point with as much force as you possibly can. You will soon find that a very definite pressure is being exerted at the point where your thumb is resting against the lectern. The harder you press the more intense the pressure becomes. At a certain point it will even be a bit painful. This pressure, when exerted as described above, will divert a good part of your thought so that you will immediately find much of your nervousness disappearing. Your mind will be divided between thinking about the pressure and thinking about the task before you. After a little while your nervousness will have passed like a current into the lectern and you will be free from any further nervousness. This can be repeated by you as many times as you may require the assistance of the lectern. As a matter of fact, you can do this every time you must speak. In leaning upon the lectern you will also find that you will have a tendency to stiffen your arms and thus put greater pressure upon the heel of the thumb by permitting your entire weight to rest on the point where it comes in contact with the sharp edge of the lectern.

What does one do if there is no lectern to lean on ? Try to arrange for a chair to be made available. If you do obtain a chair, then proceed to lean heavily upon the point of the chair at the top where the sharp edges are usually found,

Again lean as heavily as possible and hold on tight. The reaction you got when you were leaning on the sharp edge of the lectern you will get as you lean on the sharp edge of the chair.

If a desk is available, then of course you can do the same thing with the desk that you do with either the lectern or the chair. The desk can also be used in a somewhat different manner. Most desks, as we know, are very wide. It would appear extremely awkward for us to stretch our arm out wide seeking the sharp points at the edges of the desk. What we can do, however, is to open our fingers wide, place them flat upon the edge of the desk, and lean heavily upon the extended fingers. Keep the thumb out of the way since the thumb, if permitted to come to your assistance, would remove much of the weight of your body. Lean on the tips of the four fingers of each hand. Another position that can sometimes be taken on a desk is one in which you move to the side of the desk and rest all of your weight on the four fingers of the right or left hand, depending on which side of the desk you choose to use. The result will be pretty much the same. A third position that can be used at the desk in order to help relieve the tension is to sit on the edge of the desk closest to the audience. This can be done only by one who is a bit experienced but not thoroughly trained. In sitting on the edge of the desk, one foot rests on the floor and you sit on the thigh and buttock of either the right or left leg. You do not sit squarely on the desk. The only one who could possibly sit squarely on a desk facing an audience is a speaker who is thoroughly trained, who knows every trick and device in the trade, and who has that type of personality that immediately gains the confidence of the audience.

When a table is used for the speaker or chairman to lean on, the same principles follow. If the table is a narrow one

(156)

you can dig the palms of your hands into the sharp points of the table and lean heavily on it. If the table is a very wide one, then the speaker should lean upon it in the same manner as described on the desk; also the speaker may sit upon the table in exactly the same manner as was described with the desk.

Let us take another situation. There is no desk, no lectern, no table, and no chair. How can the speaker help himself to conquer that nervousness that has overcome him?

(a) Place both hands behind your back with the left thumb and the left first finger encircling the wrist of the right arm, and press very hard. This pressure will bring about the same result as the pressure experienced by the speaker when leaning on the sharp points or edges of the lectern, chair, or table. If the speaker prefers, he can encircle the left wrist in the same manner described here. It is the use of pressure to distract the mind that we are advocating. The pressure helps to do away with much of the nervousness.

(b) With both hands placed behind the back, the fingers of the left and right hand intertwine; and then you press hard, as hard as you can to create pressure points. This is not so good a position as the one described in (a) above.

(c) Speakers have been known to carry with them a small hard object which they press tightly in either the right or the left hand. This also is done for the purpose of creating pressure. Some speakers have been known to press into the middle of the palm of the hand a coin such as a quarter or a half-dollar piece. It serves the same purpose as the round hard object sometimes used.

(d) When the speaker wants to use the simplest method of all, he can entwine the fingers of both hands straight in front of him and press against the side of the body with the upper part of the arm. This is not suggested as the best method but it certainly is the simplest. It is not possible to get as much pressure from this position as from the others.

Another aid in overcoming nervousness is the use of the slow count. A speaker counts to himself or herself in a very slow manner before he or she commences. The slow count takes no more than three or four seconds, but that is enough to give one a start. Thus the speaker counts slowly to himself "one—two" and on "three" begins to talk. During this slow-count period the speaker is able to get a full view of those in front of him and at the same time take one or two good deep breaths.

Let us talk for a moment about the full view of the audience. The thing to do after getting a full view of the audience is to start out by concentrating the gaze on one or two persons until such time as the nervousness has disappeared. Of course, when the nervousness has disappeared, the speaker can act naturally and do such things as he finds to be comfortable. It is definitely an aid to pick one or two persons in the audience as the points of conversation direction.

And now, about the one or two deep breaths to which we refer. During the period of nervousness, the body is in need of oxygen, and the only way that we can get it without wearing an oxygen tank or mask is to breathe in more air. Singers are taught how to breathe. They are taught that breath control is a very important part of their method of singing. The speaker should be taught the same thing. A speaker requires a full and sufficient supply of breath to get started right. For that reason we advise the speaker to remember that it is proper and helpful for him to stop long enough to take the full breaths we are talking about.

Nervousness can be eliminated also when you, as chairman, get the feeling that you are standing upon solid ground.

(158)

The nervous individual, whether chairman or speaker, feels as though he is suspended in mid-air. The reason why he feels as though he is so suspended is the fact that he is not standing comfortably and properly. To stand comfortably and properly you must stand with both feet spread slightly apart at a distance of about one foot. Both of the toes of the shoes should be on a straight line with each other and the weight should be distributed in such a manner that no discomfort is felt at all. A speaker who is standing correctly gets the feeling that he and the floor are one unit. There is solid ground beneath his feet. He feels no distress over the lack of perfect balance. Experiment with an individual who is standing squarely on the balls of his feet. Try pushing such an individual. You will find that he cannot easily be thrown off balance and this applies to a forward or backward motion as well as to the side-to-side motion. The speaker gains confidence and even courage from this feeling of the firm ground under him. On the other hand, if the speaker does not stand correctly, and feels that he and floor are not one, there is bound to be an exaggeration of the feeling of nervousness and after a while a physical strain. Even the use of pressure may not be of much help to the speaker who feels uncomfortable in his stance.

There are lecterns and tables that have crossbars at the bottom. Sometimes these crossbars are used by chairmen and speakers to help them in their effort to find adequate aids. If you find that keeping one foot firmly planted on the floor and the other firmly planted on the crossbar of the lectern or table helps you, then by all means use this method. On the other hand, if it creates any kind of feeling of unbalance, it should definitely not be used.

And now, a final word about convincing one's self that all those persons out there in the audience are no different from

(159)

you, the chairman, or the speaker. Of course you know that they are only human beings like yourself. When they eat, they chew their food; and when they drink, they open their mouths. When they cry, they shed tears; and when they laugh, they make noises just as you do. Some of them are handsome and some are not. Some are big and some are small, and so we could go on and on pointing out the similarities between all of the persons in the audience and you as chairman or speaker. Still, you say you are inclined to be nervous. The thing then to do is to try to think of some kind of story that makes the human being appear ludicrous. When the human being appears in this light, the reaction in your mind is one that is wholly free of awe or fear. With both of these emotions removed, there is very little chance that you will be nervous. For example, if you can picture a Justice of the Supreme Court of the United States falling over a fence into a pigsty and coming up covered with muck and mire, you certainly would not be very much impressed with a spectacle of this sort. The picture in the inner mind of the cloistered chambers of the United States Supreme Court, the austere black judicial robes, and the rest of the trappings all goes out the window. He is just a sad-looking sap covered from head to foot with filthy vile-smelling mud. This approach does not necessarily mean that you look down upon the audience or that you are contemptuous. It simply means that you have come to the happy realization that there is nothing to fear. It is a known fact that the air of mystery which surrounds a strange speaker wins for him the respect of an audience. Given an individual who *is* an authority on a subject, and a member of the organization in question, and, also, given another individual who is an authority on a certain subject and who is not a member of the organization in question, you will find that the respectful attitude of

(160)

the audience is more conspicuously demonstrated toward the stranger than toward the member. The reason for this is the simple fact that the members of the organization know all about their own member-speaker. There is no mystery about him. They know that he is just like one of them. It is true that the same thing applies to the non-member speaker, but the fact still remains that the air of mystery persists.

If possible, then, try to develop the art of telling yourself about the human beings in front of you and the dull manner in which they all resemble you and one another.

The only other method that can help very much in eliminating nervousness is practice. With practice comes experience and with experience comes the escape from nervousness. Practice is gotten by being active in worthwhile organizations. Be active in worthwhile organizations because together they make up an important part of democracy. Democracy is worth working and fighting for.

Chapter 14

HOW TO BE A SUCCESSFUL CHAIRMAN

EVERY PERSON should know, as a member of an organization, how to be a chairman and at the same time have a lot of fun. If every meeting that was ruined by some incompetent half-witted chairman were laid end to end and turned into a rope, there would not be enough rope to hang every culprit responsible for ruining what otherwise might have been an enjoyable and successful evening.

You don't have to be a Venus or an Adonis to be a chairman or a chairlady. You don't have to be a Mark Twain or a declaiming Cicero. All you have to do is use a little common sense, give the subject some thought, and presto—you are the perfect chairman.

Let's get down to the business of looking into the mechanism that makes for a perfect chairman. To start with, we suggest that the following rules be strictly adhered to:

Always be thoroughly familiar with the *task* in hand. What do we mean by this? The task of being chairman, or course.

Part of the task is knowing the title of the subject discussed. If, for example, the title of the subject is "How to Treat Hysterical Mothers Who Ruin Children by Not Knowing that Children Have More Brains Than Most of Their Parents," it is wrong for the chairman to introduce the subject as "The Wrong Parents with the Brains of Children." Be sure that as a chairman you take the trouble to write down,

(162)

if necessary, the title of the subject discussed at the meeting. Don't try to improve on the title. Give it as it is given to you and let it go at that. There are times when the topic of the evening is of particular interest to you. As the chairman you are anxious to have one special phase covered. Just a moment ago we said that no chairman has the right to change the title of the talk to be given. May you do anything about it? Yes. You may as a chairman, in introducing the speaker and the subject, express the hope that a certain phase of the subject will be discussed by the speaker. For example, if the speaker is going to talk about international affairs and you are the chairman, and it happens that you are particularly interested in the Mongolian situation, it is perfectly proper for you to say as part of your introduction, "And I do hope that the speaker will have an opportunity to touch upon the Mongolian question." That's enough. You have made your point and the speaker, if he knows what he is about, will try to accommodate you. If he doesn't, it is just too bad.

A very good example of just how a well-intentioned person can make a grand mess of a meeting as a chairlady occurred a short time ago. This chairlady did not know the task before her.

At a meeting of a parent-teachers association, a very prominent child-psychologist had been invited to make the principal address of the evening. A certain person, whom we will call Mrs. Fluff, was the chairlady. Mrs. Fluff had read many books on child psychology and how to bring up children, and she felt that there was almost nothing about the subject of child psychology that she did not feel thoroughly qualified to discuss. She herself had listened to almost every well-known lecturer and she never failed to attend those famous $5O-a-plate-conferences among the elite in the field of psychology. The time came when Mrs. Fluff had to introduce

(163)

the principal speaker of the evening. Before the meeting got under way it had been understood that the speaker would be given the floor at 9:30. After the lecture there was to be a question period and then a short discussion from the floor. The meeting was to be adjourned at 11 P.M. The committee in charge had learned from past experience that a successful meeting must end at a reasonably early hour. An early adjournment makes it possible for persons living at a distance to get home before their eyes are shut tight by sleepy lids. Men and women who must go to work daily like to be in bed before midnight. Women as a rule do not like to be about without an escort after midnight. All these things had been carefully considered by the committee in charge.

True it is that Mrs. Fluff knew her subject, but it is also true that by the time she wound up her more than 20-minute introduction of the speaker, she had covered a good part of the subject herself, and had even raised a number of controversial questions by statements she had made. During the agonizing period of waiting for the chairlady to conclude, the audience became restless and nervous. The speaker did everything but froth at the mouth, and the net result of this situation was a meeting that left a bad taste with every person in attendance.

Here you have an example of a person who knew the *subject* to be discussed, but did not know the task in hand. Remember! The task is that of being a chairman or chairlady —that is the first rule.

2. Another rule to remember is: HAVE MORE THAN A VAGUE IDEA ABOUT THE SUBJECT TO BE DISCUSS-ED. If you will examine this phrase very carefully, you will notice that it is different from the rule we referred to above. Here we are urging you as chairman to know something about the subject as well as the *task*. If, like Mrs. Fluff, you

(164)

are interested in the subject, and for your own pleasure you want to become expert, that's all right. By all means do so, but don't do what Mrs. Fluff did. On the other hand, if you are going to be the chairman of the meeting at which the discussion will be on the topic of "The Age of Dinosaur Eggs in the Gobi Desert and Modern Art," you should make it your business to find out what sort of eggs are dinosaur eggs, what a dinosaur is, where the Gobi Desert is located, and a thing or two about modern art. That's enough! YOU ARE NOT REQUIRED AS A CHAIRMAN TO BE AN EXPERT IN THE FIELD RELATING TO THE SUBJECT BEING DISCUSSED AT THE MEETING. We repeat. Know something about the subject and the task, and you will be fulfilling two of the requirements of a perfect chairman. Here is an example of what is meant by knowing the subject. At a meeting of the board of an orphanage asylum, the chairman was chosen to preside over the meeting solely because the citizens of that community had chosen her husband as their Representative in Congress. The combined brains of the chairlady and her husband may not have been superior to that of a high-grade moron. Most people being hero worshippers, however, the members were proud of the fact that Mrs. Woodenhead, the wife of Representative Woodenhead, was going to be the chairlady. She opened the meeting by gushing forth with a lot of sentimental drivel about the heart-breaking conditions facing parentless orphans. She went on and on, making matters worse and worse. The lady completely ruined the meeting. The orphanage that had invited her to be the chairlady was in reality not an orphanage, even though it was called that. The children who lived in the home had at least one parent living, and in some instances had both parents living. In most cases one of the parents was in some sort of institution. Mrs. Woodenhead

(165)

did not take the time or the trouble to find out what sort of institution it was that had invited her to be chairlady. She had seen the word "orphanage" and, in her mind, that was all she needed. Mrs. Woodenhead knew how to be drippingly sentimental and, by Jove, she was going to ring their hearts for them! Mrs. Woodenhead was lucky she didn't get her neck wrung for her (it is our opinion that the good people who still run the orphanage have probably not learned a lesson yet).

A little bit of time, a little bit of care, and a note or two on a little card will help you immensely in making sure that you do know the subject and that you don't behave as described above.

A classic example of an attempt by an individual to act as a chairman is the following:

Setting: A classroom in a university in the state of New York.
Subject: A discussion of the play Ibsen's *Ghosts*.
Time: The year 1950.

A university student is acting as chairman of a group of fellow students supposed to be drama critics. Each student has been given a title and a newspaper or magazine he is supposed to represent. The chairman opens up as follows,

Ghosts by Ibsen

Since this is the first time that I am giving a report on a play and being no Danton Walker or Conrad Nagel I will have to do this in shall we say laymen's terms. As far as the writing and the putting across the play the workshop did an admirable job. But in seeing the play many questions were left unanswered by the way the play was put across. It seem-

(166)

ed that in the shortening down which the group did do to put it across in such a short time, they seemed to leave out the essence and the background of the play. Not being sure of whether the play is supposed to be presented in an in-the-round manner or not, I might recommend that if possible that future plays be presented in the regular manner presented—that is, on a stage. I may have this complaint although because I happened to have picked or shown to a seat facing the backs of all the players.

About the players: I personally felt that all the players seemed to feel that they had a show to put over and did a real job. None of them of course showing real polish although. In several places they spoke so low that I, sitting no more than ten feet from them, could hardly hear them. I also felt that the pace at which they went was terrific. I think that if a short spell were given the players and the audience during the first part a little more interest and a lot more finer setting might have been presented. A little rest for the weary (that is, the players and the students) might have helped.

Another thing which I might criticize since that's what I'm doing anyhow is that the lights be shielded and taken out of the audience's eyes so that they may not have to be such a distraction.

But as far as an evening of enjoyment to which I would not have ordinarily gone since during the last week of studying for exams, it was fine and I think that feeling was shared by all. We will call on Jonathan now to start making a report on his version of the play.

(This is a verbatim report and has not been edited at all. It is the chairman's introduction of the subject and the first speaker.)

(167)

3. NEVER TAKE MORE THREE OR FOUR MINUTES TO INTRODUCE ANY SPEAKER.

Every living being who has ever attended a meeting is able to tell of at least one instance where a chairman started out to introduce a speaker at 9 o'clock and didn't finish that introduction until maybe 9:15 or 9:20 (it is our hope that some day there will be a law justifying the shooting on sight of any such chairmen). Always bear in mind that people come to see and listen to the speaker or speakers and not to the chairman. No one has the right to stand up front like a half-mad peacock strutting its beautiful plumes just because some individuals were unfortunate enough to make him chairman. If you are "The Chair," use your head and do things in a simple and intelligent manner. Yes, in a simple manner. When you have to introduce a speaker, plan your introduction so that you can say everything that should be said within a period of two or three minutes, maybe four, but never more. How do you do it? Remember the following and you will always be safe:

(a) The speaker's full name. *Be sure* to find out whether it is Miss or Mrs.; whether it is Dr. or Professor, whether it is Reverend, Rabbi, Monsignor, or Brother. If you don't know the proper title, ask the speaker before you do the introducing. Write it down. Avoid the embarrassment of stopping in the middle of an introduction and saying to a lady, "Is it Miss or Mrs.?" It is discourteous, unintelligent, and even unkind for a chairman to do such a thing. It is so simple to ask a person exactly what the title is preceding the name. You have no idea how unhappy an individual is when he is introduced as Professor Muttontop when he knows that he is only an instructor, and it will probably be 20 years before he becomes a professor. All right, then, you know the speaker's full name and title.

(168)

(b) What field of endeavor is the speaker prominent in? If he happens to be a podiatrist, don't introduce him as a leading pediatrician. Check up and make sure that his field of activity is fully and properly described to you. Don't depend on some tongue-wagging gossip to supply the information. Get it from a reliable source. Get it from the speaker or from a book that will *give* you information about the speaker. If necessary, call the speaker's office. If he has no office, call his home. If he has no home and no office, and no books that tell you anything about him, wait until you see him or her at the meeting, and ask the speaker point-blank for some biographical material. It takes only a moment or two to get the information. Even if the meeting is late and the pressure is great, take time out to get the facts. Ask the speaker how he or she would like to be introduced. You can make money betting that the more scholarly and important the individual, the more modest the introduction will be.

The story is told of a very eminent mathematician and astronomer who was once asked by a chairlady, "How would you prefer to be introduced, sir?" and the scholar immediately answered, "Just tell them I am a star gazer." She did exactly as she was asked and the audience was very pleased by the simplicity and modesty of the lecturer. It so happens that this astronomer had written many books and articles. The audience knew a great deal about him. They were persons who had spent many years in the field of mathematics and astronomy. He was the dean of them all, yet his preferred introduction was so simple and beautiful. The chair-lady of this meeting was very wise. She told the audience the following: "I was prepared to make a very lengthy introduction of our next speaker. It was my intention to give you only a part of the long list of books written by our guest and to tell you only a little bit about the honors and awards that have been bestowed upon him. He has himself, however, summed up the manner of introducing him by expressing a preference for the description star gazer. I now have the honor of introducing the world-renowned authority in astronomy, Professor S_____, a star gazer." If you examine this introduction, you will find that the chairlady very cleverly used every trick and device available to one who knows the business. This chairlady had gone to the trouble of knowing a little bit about the subject at hand as well as the task. She knew that the speaker was an eminent authority who had written many books and articles and that the speaker had received honors and awards from many governments throughout the world. She also knew that people in the audience were conversant with the subject and the professor's accomplishments; still the chairlady was conscious of the fact that something should be added to the professor's request—something that would hint at all of the honors and the authoritative words of the professor, without going into too great detail. If the chairlady had attempted to show off all that she knew about the professor, many persons in the audience would have resented such presumption, while on the other hand the very diplomatic manner in which the Chair handled the situation resulted in a warm response from the audience to the chairlady and the speaker as well. Notice how short the introduction was and how packed-full of information. The chairlady started out by telling the audience what she originally had in mind. She said, "I was prepared to make a lengthy, factual introduction . . . "In that short phrase, she told the audience (a) that she had prepared herself to act as chairlady; (b) that she had taken the trouble to find out many facts about the speaker; (c) that the chairlady considered her job an important one; and (d) that her introduction would have given many facts, but she, the chair-

(170)

lady, took it for granted that it would not be necessary for her to do so because the speaker was going to do a good job and, further, because she, the chairlady, felt that many persons in the audience did not need any recital of facts concerning the speaker. Immediately she won the confidence and the gratitude of the audience. They were flattered by the idea that the chairlady indicated to them that she took her position seriously, thus reflecting an attitude of respect toward the audience:

Now let us take another look at this introduction. "It was my intention to *give* you only a part of the long list of books written by our guest and to tell you only a little bit about the honors and awards bestowed upon him." What has the chairlady done here? She has very carefully abbreviated what could have been a long and nauseating oration, full of flattery concerning a person who deserved to be flattered, but who most certainly did not care for it. The chairlady let it be known that there was a "long list of books written by our guest." See how the Chair has told the audience a great deal in only a few words. Try to imagine in your own mind how many hundreds of words she could have used in naming the books written by the professor and telling what the books were about, and possibly telling how well the books were received. No, she didn't do that. She used a better method. She started out by making a broad statement and then left it to the audience to fill in the gaps. She described the list of books written by the professor as a "long list." What does that bring to mind to the listener? The answer is simple. Immediately, the listener has a picture in his mind of a shelf of books, each one of them bearing the name of the speaker about to be introduced. That gives him a position of importance and, in most instances, that is right. In contrast to the use of the term "long list of books," the speaker

(171)

referred to the fact that she was going to tell "only a little bit about the honors and awards bestowed on the speaker." Notice the very clever use of contrasts. Even though they are opposites, they both give the same impression. When the chairlady said she was going to tell only "a little bit" about the honors, the listeners had another picture in their minds, namely, that of medals and citations and honorary degrees. It may very well be that the listeners in the audience even bestowed more honors and awards upon the professor than he had actually ever received, but that should not deter any chairman or chairlady from using this sort of approach. The chairlady told the truth. She is not responsible if the listeners are so generous in their interpretation of what she said. The chairlady was "warming up the audience." This she did by her very fine and short introduction.

Once more, we return to the introduction. The chairlady has let the audience in on a little personal touch. She has told them about that private conversation between herself and the speaker. Again the chairlady has used a very good device in bringing the audience and the speaker closer together. The chairlady has told the audience about the speaker's modesty when she said, "He has himself, however, summed up the manner of introducing him by expressing a preference for the description star gazer." This strikes a responsive chord in the minds of the listening audience. They like the idea that so eminent a person is so modest in his description of himself. Combine this with the fact that the chairlady told them that the professor had personally expressed such a preference and you get the picture of the projection of a speaker's personality to the audience even before the speaker commences.

We come now to the final sentence in the chairlady's intro-duction. She said, "I now have the honor of introducing the

world-renowned authority in astronomy, Professor S_____,
a star gazer." The chairlady by this sentence has said in substance to the speaker and to the audience, "I have been honored
by being permitted to be in this position of chairlady." It is
gracious on the part of the Chair to indicate to the speaker that
the Chair is flattered by the honor bestowed upon her and, in
Minding up, she puts it very succinctly by describing the
speaker in one phrase as "the world-renowned authority in
astronomy." Here you have an excellent example of what to do
and how to do it when you are in the chair. BUT DON'T
THINK THAT THIS IS ALL THERE IS TO IT. ALL WE ARE
DOING IS GIVING YOU AN EXAMPLE OF SOMETHING
THAT CAN BE OF GREAT HELP.

Don't get to thinking that it is as easy to introduce all per
sons as it is to introduce Professor S_____. There are mil
lions of little persons who love big introductions.

Maybe you don't like it any more than we do, but we must
face reality and must talk about what a chairman or chairlady
should do in introducing the person who loves flattery. Now
you have a real problem. Let's sink our teeth into it immediately. Remember what we said before. Be sure that you
have the speaker's full name, his full title, and that you know
how to pronounce correctly the speaker's name. Here we go; we
are about to introduce this strutting rooster who thinks that the
sun has to rise and set on him. He is nothing but a hollow log
and a puffed-up windbag, but you are the chairman and you are
stuck with him, so what can you do since you are not allowed to
shoot him out of season? You find out that Mr. Swallowtail
was once upon a time the past Exalted High Potentate of the
Order of Puddenheads. His ancestors were one of the million
or more who came over on the *Mayflower.* His wife was the
well-known Effie Goose-feather, head of the Ladies'
Auxiliary of the former Revolu-

(173)

tionary Sons of Bath. Mr. Swallowtail is also chairman of the committee to raise funds for the education of the Chinese Boy Scouts and a contributor to the Society of Mummified Egyptologists. Well, that's all we can say about this bore who is going to address the society of which you are the chairman. What to do, what to do! Don't let it get you. Make your introduction something like this: "Ladies and gentlemen, and members of the Excruciating Society, this is the fifth in the winter series of talks to be given under the auspices of the Committee on Education of our Society. Each week, we invite a different speaker to talk with us on the topic of 'The Mystical or the Metaphysical,' and today we continue this interesting series by having as our speaker a citizen of extraordinarily important stature in the community. He was, as you know, chairman of————; he is now the chairman of————; he is a member of A Club, B Club, and Indian Club; he has lectured widely on the subject we are about to hear and I know that his talk will continue the thrilling experiences we have had in the previous four meetings of our society. I would consider myself remiss in my duties as chairman on this auspicious occasion if I failed to mention that the former Effie Goosefeather, the head of blah, blah, blah, is none other than the wife of our distinguished speaker. And now it gives me pleasure to introduce the speaker of the evening who will talk on the subject of 'The Mystical or the Metaphysical,' Mr. John Swallowtail." Always give the name last.

You've done your job even though it almost killed you. Introducing this nonentity required more effort than moving a mountain. Contrast this introduction with the introduction given to Professor S. Mr. Swallowtail has no substance to him. He is of such little consequence that the little things re-

(174)

lating to him must be magnified in order to give the impression that they are big.

We go back for a moment to take apart your introduction. You are not too happy about your job, but you do want to be formal and courteous. You therefore address the audience thus: "Ladies and gentlemen, and members of the Excruciating Society." Now you have made your proper formal opening. You recite the fact that there is a series of lectures and that this series of lectures is the winter series. For those members who have been fortunate enough not to attend, you advise them that they have escaped the first four orgies of agony. This you have done in your sentence, "This is the fifth in the winter series of talks." What else have you done? You have given credit to the little minds who would be offended if you did not mention that their Committee on Education is the one which guides the cultural activities of the Society. The next thing you did was to describe when these meetings take place and how the Society runs them and for what purpose. All this is contained in the sentence, "Each week we invite a different speaker (thank goodness!) to talk with us on the topic of____." These are facts and they give a description of the program. This is the point at which you have got to swallow hard and begin introducing someone who is no one. You have puffed up his little accomplishments, so that they sound important. You have done the best you can with little material. There is only one thing you have done that would put the speaker at a disadvantage, and that is, you have told him that the previous four meetings were thrilling. That may make the speaker nervous. It is best not to use any descriptive terminology about any other speakers or lectures or meetings. The thing to do is make the statement that you know the speaker will carry on the successful talks that preceded the one he is about to deliver. One last shot—you have touched his ego and flattered him and his wife by referring to the fact that his wife is the former Miss so-and-so and this presupposes an important status in "society."

This is the point at which every chairman should be told about and drilled on the rule: DON'T LAY IT ON TOO THICK. You know what we mean. Let's go back a moment to the introduction of Mr. Swallowtail. Imagine what your embarrassment would be if you had introduced that nincompoop as a scholar and the best this, the most experienced that, and the world-famed so and so? You would find yourself in a position where all the wrath of the audience would be vented upon your head (and in our opinion, justly so). So again, we admonish you: DON'T LAY IT ON TOO THICK.

Don't look now, but we are going to *give* you an exception to the rule: DON'T LAY IT ON TOO THICK. Sometimes you do find a human being who is a genuine scholar and who does know what in the world he is talking about and he really is an important fellow in his own field, but strangely enough he loves to be introduced by a chairman who hands out the taffy in very thick rolls. Yes, believe it or not, there are some brilliant people who like the flattery laid on heavily. Give it to them. Pick up every little piece of information concerning the speaker's accomplishments and recite it to your audience. However, do not deviate from the rule that your introduction is to take two or three minutes and never more than four.

Sit yourself down for a moment and pretend that you are going to introduce Sir Oswald De Camp Schmaltz, an authority on English history. He is a Fellow of the Royal Academy, a full professor of history at two universities simultaneously; he has written eleven books, has four degrees and a number of honorary titles. He has lectured in every important university in the world and has been decorated as a member of the household of the Kingdom of Tutt and is One of the Boys in the Royal Society of the King's Garter as well as a High Potentate in the Society of the Queen's Wig. Add another dozen or so unnecessary appendages. You are going to face the prospect of introducing this mogul. Can you do so in three or four minutes? You most certainly can. Start out as follows: "Distinguished guests, members and friends of the Research Society, ladies and gentlemen: in the course of a lifetime, *it* rarely falls to the lot of any one citizen acting as a chairman to be placed in the position of introducing so distinguished a speaker as the one I wish to present to you. He is a member of the Royal Society, etc., etc., and 31 more etceteras."

Get yourself a stop watch and go through this tomfoolery and see whether we are right when we say that all of this bunk can be ladeled out as heavily as frozen gravy in three minutes or even less. Get going friend, and try it. When you have convinced yourself, you have learned a great deal more about how to be a perfect chairman.

Chapter 15

RIGHTS, DUTIES, PRIVILEGES OF A CHAIRMAN, AND A FEW DONT'S

BY THIS TIME it should be pretty clear to anyone that being chairman is a job that needs a diplomat, a parliamentarian, a psychologist and a generally well-balanced individual. The discussion up to this point has been limited to the chairman of a meeting in which no organization business is transacted. It would be unfortunate if this book were to end without some words about being a chairman at a business meeting. What follows is a very much condensed outline. To write in detail about a chairman at a business meeting would require a volume once again as big as this one and maybe even more —and it would certainly have to be a volume much less readable or understandable than this one. Please, dear reader, don't get the idea you know it all because you have memorized this chapter. It just ain't so. This is only a small crutch for you to lean on.

HINTS TO CHAIRMEN

(1) Always refer to yourself as "The Chair." Theoretically a chairman is supposed to be able to be absolutely objective, scrupulously honest, and capable of handling every situation on every occasion. Thus a chairman runs "The Chair" on an impersonal level. The term "The Chair" adds to the illusion of the impersonal. The members of the organ-

(178)

ization can feel freer in their discussions and differences with the chairman when they have the feeling that the chairman is a symbol and not an individual who may give or receive offense by any remarks that may be made. Remember then always to use the term "The Chair."

Psychologically the human being is inclined to resent the power of anyone in authority. The burden of law and its restrictions is something that all men at one time or another want to cast off, even if it is only for a brief period of time. When the chairman uses the pronoun "I," the reaction in the mind of every member is generally an antagonistic one. Even though he doesn't say so and may not consciously feel it, the unspoken reaction is something like this: "I don't care how you feel or what you think. I am interested in the judgment of the Chair and not you."

Imagine a business session in which a chairman is making a ruling on a point of order. He is going to rule against the member raising the point of order and he says, "I rule the point of order is not well taken." This is wrong for two reasons. First, the chairman always refers to himself as "The Chair"; and second, the member who raised the point of order gets the feeling, "Oh you do, eh? Well I don't care much about your personal feelings. Confine your rulings to those of chairman and leave out this I business." It is much easier for a member to be overruled by a chairman who softens the blow by using the term "The Chair rules . . ." than "I rule ..."

(2) Always stand up while (a) "stating" or "putting" a question that is to be debated; (b) whenever a vote is being taken; (c) when a ruling is being made or explained; (d) when information is being given at the request of a member.

In all of the instances just set forth the chairman is carrying on the business of the meeting. In meetings where parliamentary rules and laws are observed, the chairman is required to stand while addressing the members or actively guiding the proceedings on their way to a conclusion. It is also common courtesy to stand up under such circumstances. The chairman should be standing up because he must at all times have the meeting under his gaze. He must be prepared to recognize any member who wishes to be recognized (if the member is then in order). It has a much greater effect upon the members when the chairman is standing before them than when he transacts business from a sitting position. He seems to be indifferent and almost bored when he undertakes to carry on while sitting down.

(3) Be seated during debate. A debate can be conducted only when the speakers are permitted to have the floor by the chairman—in other words, one may not speak unless he is in order. Once the chairman gives the floor to a member, only that member has the right thereto and that means that even the chairman should be seated and paying attention. All eyes are supposed to be focused on the speaking member. A standing chairman is distracting, unless he is working at some thing set forth in Paragraph 2. Nothing should be done or permitted to be done that in any wise deprives a member of the right to the floor and the attention of all present.

(4) A chairman should take part in debates only on rare occasions. The chairman does not give up his right to take part in any debates simply because he is the chairman. If he is a member of the assembly, he has the same rights as any other member. Bear in mind that one who becomes a chair man acquires certain rights and privileges and gives up some others. While the chairman does have the right to take part in debates, he should remember that he is expected to be absolutely impartial and show no signs of prejudice. When he argues for or against a particular point of view, he shows

his hand and the opposing side becomes suspicious of the chairman's actions or motives thereafter. If the chairman insists upon entering the debate, he should relinquish the Chair until the matter under discussion is disposed of. If his participation in the debate is of minor significance and he has not indicated his attitude on the whole question before the house, he may resume his position as chairman or even remain in the Chair while exercising his right to be heard.

(5) Never interrupt a speaker unless it is absolutely necessary. As was stated before, once a member has been duly recognized and given the floor, no one may interrupt him except for some proper or lawful reason. A chairman in this respect has no greater right than any member of the assembly. If the chairman does not agree with the speaker, it is just too bad. The chairman may interrupt only if the speaker is out of order, abusive, or taking up more than the allotted time. He may also interrupt a speaker in order to recognize a member seeking to be heard for good cause. In an emergency the chairman may always interrupt.

(6) Dress neatly. No loud clothes or accessories. A chairman is in a conspicuous position. He has a difficult job. To carry on with a minimum of resistance he must have the undivided attention of the members and cause no distraction himself. Because the chairman is in such a conspicuous position, the members immediately notice any thing that is extraordinary. Ties that almost glare, shirts of a pastel hue, shoes that only a hero would dare wear, or a sparkling diamond are bound to keep the members buzzing and distracted. Dress neatly, plainly, and in good taste. It helps a great deal.

(7) Never smoke while presiding at a meeting. Smoking is neither a crime nor a vice, but it is out of place when indulged in by a chairman. The rule is: avoid distraction. Does smoking distract? It does. Visualize the chairman fiddling

with a package of cigarettes, ripping away at the stubborn cellophane. Finally he gets a cigarette out and strikes a match after fumbling through his pockets—he may have one of those cigarette lighters that never seems to function. All this is distracting, time-wasting, and irritating to those who wait for the chairman to light up. Now he must draw a good full puff. His voice is muffled in smoke belching forth from mouth and nose. It is indeed a weak man who cannot keep from smoking for a short hour or two while presiding at a meeting. If the chairman must smoke he should ask the vice-chairman or next-ranking officer to take over temporarily. This is the easiest way out.

(8) Never chew gum or candy. This hint needs very little elaboration. It is considered bad manners to chew in public, and it is particularly so at meetings. A chairman who chews while presiding antagonizes those sitting before him.

(9) Be a diplomat at all times, even when you are very angry. A chairman is always in the middle of every conflict. He cannot escape this position. Being a human being, he has ideas of his own; but being a chairman, he must put aside his opinions and help steer the business of the organization along channels that are clear of obstacles. In his remarks he must use just the right words and avoid offending anyone. He must not permit a member to goad him into rash action. When the other fellow gets hot and excited, the chairman speaks softly and avoids sarcasm or expressions of antagonism or insult. The firm quiet manner wins support from members. Never shout or make gestures that indicate disgust or a threat. Everyone likes a gentleman. A gentleman is a good diplomat. Bend backwards to be a gentleman.

(10) Always pay strict attention. It is the duty of a chairman to know everything that is going on. In order to rule correctly, he must have a complete picture and understand-

ing of the proceedings. This he can do only by paying strict attention. Another reason why a chairman must pay strict attention is the fact that every member who gets the floor is entitled to the attention of everyone present. And that means the chairman too.

Once a chairman loses track of what is going on he is bound to cause confusion. The resulting confusion will put the meeting beyond the chairman's control to such a degree that in short order the meeting will wind up in one grand mess.

(11) A few don'ts for chairman:

Many chairmen are guilty of a grave fault. It seems that they lose themselves in anger and begin to scold the audience that is present because many people who were expected to or who should have come failed to put in an appearance. Isn't it strange to find yourself in front of a chairman who keeps bawling out the audience that did come? On and on he goes, berating more and more, instead of being kind and thankful to those who did show up. Remember, then, that as a chairman, you never, never scold those who are present. Praise them, thank them, and be happy.

When an audience is a small one it isn't necessary for the chairman to keep reminding those present that the lack of numbers is a keen disappointment. If you're the chairman don't get the foolish idea that only you count. Take bets that in an audience of 150 there are at least 5 who can count as well as you do, and furthermore they are just as capable as you are of understanding and seeing that the audience is a small one.

Instead of wailing and complaining, be brave and a good sport. Try to laugh it off. Make excuses if you can, but do it in short swift sentences and then drop it. Make up in interest and warmth what the meeting lacks in number.

In every audience there is almost always at least one person or maybe even more whom you know personally. They may be neighbors or relatives or friends. So what ? Must you wave to them and nod and distract the people in the audience and cause them to stare and gape and try to find out who it is you are waving at and nodding to ? You can always acknowledge the presence of those you know by the slightest semblance of a smile and an unnoticeable nod as you look directly at the one you wish to greet. That is all. Pay attention to your meeting.

Some chairmen think it is all right to use slang or even swear words at public meetings. It is not. There is something about a chairman that makes him for the time being a person apart in the eyes of the audience. The chairman is expected to be a perfect gentleman. There is an aura about him that may not be destroyed without spoiling the meeting. Even to the roughest, toughest guy in the world, there is an aversion to the words "hell" or "damn" when uttered by a chairman. It just is not in keeping with the way a chairman is expected to conduct himself. Does it make any difference if the meeting is a stuffed-shirt lecture or a polyglot mass meeting or a shop meeting? It does not. The same psychological reaction takes place on all occasions. Therefore, never, never stray from the straight and narrow. It always helps. It never hurts. Don't swear—don't use slang expressions.

Don't be discouraged about this chairman business. There's more to come that is encouraging. It's still fun to be a chairman.

RIGHTS OF A CHAIRMAN

(1) He may demand that all main motions and resolutions be written out before they are formally presented.

This is done when the chairman finds that a very controversial matter is about to become the subject of debate. One word this way or that, even though innocently misquoted, may bring on a torrent of abuse, accusations, and much unnecessary wrangling. The chairman therefore takes no chances and insists that the main motion be written out. The chairman is the one who *states* the motion after it is made. He repeats it for the secretary to record. When it is written out no mistake can occur. Writing out a main motion or resolution also simplifies the process of amending the motion or modifying the resolution.

(2) The chairman may rule on motions when made, without waiting for any member to raise a point of order. If, in the opinion of the chairman, the motion or anything subsequent to it is out of order, he can stop the proceedings and insist that the errors be corrected. Only he can exercise such power. In conjunction with this right he may interrupt a speaker who is drifting away from the point at issue, insulting another member, or acting in a disorderly manner.

(3) He is the one who recognizes the member entitled to the floor. He may, of course, be overruled by the members if he is challenged on the question of who rightfully is en titled to the floor. In his position, the chairman, by using his prerogatives, can help advance his point of view without being unfair or prejudiced. If a given proposition is on the floor for debate and ultimate vote, and the chairman is anxious to have his point of view prevail, he will recognize speakers in such order that the debate by members favoring his side will proceed from weakness to strength. The chair man recognizes in the course of debate a member who can present a fair argument for the chairman's point of view. He may follow with a member who is weaker and keep in reserve the strongest speaker for his side. This tactic is pro-

per and is recognized as the legitimate way in which a chairman can help get his point of view across. In addition to the above, he may recognize the opposition's strongest speakers first and wind up with their weakest.

Where a chairman does not have strong views on a matter, he gets a great feeling of satisfaction when he has successfully guided a matter through debate and no complaints have been made against his conduct. As far as possible he should remain neutral.

(4) A chairman may vote in the event of a tie. In all cases where a tie vote results, the chairman may cast a vote to break the tie. He is not deprived of the right to vote simply because he is the chairman.

(5) He may vote to sustain a ruling of the chair after an appeal has been taken. Many people are under the mis taken impression that a chairman may not vote to sustain his own ruling. This is not so. He may and should vote to sustain his ruling unless he has become convinced that he made an error in his ruling or if he purposely wanted an ad verse ruling by the body in order to settle a question of law. It should also be borne in mind that a chairman vacates the chair in order to permit an appeal to be heard. He calls up the vice-chairman or other qualified officer to take over during the argument on the appeal. It is the acting chairman who is carrying on when voting on the appeal takes place; therefore he may vote without any question as to propriety or right.

(6) He may vote to make a tie. A chairman may cast his vote to make a tie. Again we repeat, a chairman may vote at all times if he is a member of the assembly. If he wants a matter defeated and his vote will do so, there is nothing wrong in his casting his vote to make a tie. He has

DUTIES OF A CHAIRMAN

as much right to exercise his right to vote as any other member.

(7)   He may vote to uphold or defeat a two-thirds vote. In a number of instances parliamentary rules require a vote of two-thirds of those present to pass or defeat a given motion. When the vote is taken and it is found that the voting is short one vote of two-thirds, the chairman may cast his vote to supply the needed number; and of course he may do the exact opposite, namely, cast his one vote against the total and defeat the proposition.

(8)   He may vote whenever his vote will affect the result, unless the vote is by secret ballot. Two things appear obvious here. One is that it is useless and senseless for a chairman to vote and thus disclose his attitude, when his vote will in no wise affect the result; and the other is that a secret ballot is a very important matter. The secret ballot is one of the greatest assets of a free people and its value is never to be deprecated or minimized; thus when the voting is by secret ballot, the chairman may not wait until the votes have been cast and counted and then cast his ballot in order to make or break a tie or a two-thirds vote. The secret ballot is secret for the chairman as well as all other members. There is no room for any exception to the rule.

(9)   He may refuse to accept frivolous or dilatory motions. Every now and then some member at a business meeting will act up. He will think he is being funny by offering some sort of silly or frivolous motion—that is, a motion that makes no sense or has no bearing on anything at all. A dilatory motion is one that is made to kill time or block progess or cause confusion.   A well-trained and wide-awake chairman can easily recognize such motions and he is with in his rights in refusing to recognize them. Every member

should back a chairman who has the good sense and courage to rule out such motions. Sometimes a chairman who is inclined to be dictatorial or brazen will rule a motion out on these grounds even though it is not so. In such a case every member should jump on the chairman and teach him to mind his p's and q's.

(10) He may declare debate closed when no more members wish to be heard. This he does only after affording members a reasonable opportunity to ask for the floor. The chairman need not wait for a motion to close debate under such circumstances. He moves on to the next step in the business at hand.

(11) Where a motion has once been lost and an attempt is made to renew the motion with the obvious intent of obstructing the progress of the business, the chairman may refuse to recognize the attempted re-introduction of the mot ion.

The following is a good example of such a trick: A motion is made and seconded that the organization spend $1,000,000.00 on spinning tops. After debate it is defeated 151 to 2. A new item of business is then taken up and disposed of. The maker of the first motion gets up and moves that the body go on record recommending the purchase of spinning tops and that the sum of $1,000,000.00 be appropriated therefore. The Chair rules the motion out of order. The Chair is correct. This motion can do nothing but obstruct business—it has already been voted down overwhelmingly at this session.

(12) He may refuse to entertain the same point of order made more than once in the same session. When a point of order is raised and the chairman rules the point of order not well taken, that finishes the objection unless an appeal is taken. If an appeal is taken and the Chair is sustained,

then the ruling of the Chair becomes the law relating to the motion. If the person who originally raised the point of order soon gets up again and raises the same objection, or if anyone else gets up and raises the same objection, the Chair may refuse to recognize the objection.

For example: A motion is made and seconded to charge additional dues of $1.00 per month. A point of order is raised that the motion violates the constitution of the organization. The chairman rules the point of order not well taken. The member takes an appeal—the members sustain the Chair and the meeting goes on. In a few minutes a different member (or even the member who was overruled) gets up and raises the point of order that the motion violates the constitution of the organization. The chairman refuses to recognize the point of order because it has just been raised and ruled on. The chairman is again correct.

(13) He can order a rising vote when in doubt. All votes are taken and announced by the chairman and no one else. Most votes are voice votes {viva voce, they are called), but there are occasions when the vote is taken by a show of hands. If the Chair finds neither method satisfactory, he may order the voting members to stand and be counted. He needs no authorization to order a rising vote. A member may demand a hand vote or any other method by which an exact count can be had.

DUTIES OF THE CHAIR

(1) The chairman calls the meeting or session to order. In all organizations governed by parliamentary rules it is the chairman who calls members to order. He is the symbol of authority. When the chairman is present no one else may call the meeting to order.

(2) The chairman makes rulings. Whenever a point of order is raised the chairman *must* make a ruling. He has no alternative. Making rulings is part of his business. Only when the point of order is withdrawn and no objection is raised may the chairman avoid ruling.

(3) The chairman *states* motions. This is one of the most misunderstood phases of parliamentary law. An example is the best way to explain what is meant by *stating* a motion. Member A gets the floor. He makes a motion that is second ed. The chairman recites the motion to the secretary. When the secretary has written the motion into the minute book the chairman turns to the members and *repeats* the motion. This is known as *stating* the motion. Until the chairman "states" the motion there can be no debate.

(4) In some societies where the chairman is also the president, he, together with the secretary, signs the minutes. Where the minutes are published they are always signed by the president and secretary.

(5) He appoints tellers to count the votes and he announces the result. Only the chairman may do this. When ever a hand or standing vote is to be taken, the chairman ap points tellers to do the counting. As each teller finishes his part of the counting, he reports to the secretary. The secretary adds them all up and reports to the chairman. *The chair man announces the result of the voting.*

(6) He announces the agenda for the day and the order in which the business is to be acted on. His announced agenda is subject to acceptance or modification or rejection by the membership. As a general rule, the agenda as announced by the chairman is accepted. In most organizations the agenda is a standing and regular order of business and the announcement of the chairman is only *pro forma.*

(7) The chairman may adjourn the meeting in case of an

emergency without waiting for the consent of the assembly. During the war there were many occasions when meetings were adjourned by the chairman because of sudden blackouts. If a riot breaks out the chairman may adjourn the meeting and not wait for it to be broken up.

(8) The chairman always declares the meeting adjourned in due time. When it is the will of the membership that the meeting be adjourned, the chairman is the one who announces, "This meeting stands adjourned." Only he has the right to make this announcement.

APPENDIX

One of the problems an organization frequently has to face is: How should a letter be addressed to a public servant or a member of the clergy or a member of the armed forces when inviting a speaker from one of the organizations just referred to?

Another problem is the one a chairman faces in introducing a member of the clergy or a public servant or a member of the armed forces, etc.

Listed below is part of the explanation of the problem referred to above. For the purpose of making things simple, the correct form of address to be used in a letter is set forth; also the manner in which the letter is to commence. Whenever there are alternate ways of addressing or commencing the letter, all the alternatives are set forth. The same things have been done to aid the chairman when he introduces a speaker.

The important personages who may at some time or other be invited are listed below and appear in their alphabetical order:

To address a letter to an alderman or city councilman, the letter should commence as follows:
Alderman John Tin,
City Hall,
Brookville, N. Y.
Dear Sir:

or

City Councilman John Stone, City Hall, Brookville, N. Y. Dear Sir:

Please note that the letters commence with the terms "Dear Sir." Other forms are not acceptable.

A chairman in introducing an alderman or city councilman may use any one of the following terms:

"I now have the pleasure to introduce to you (or the honor to introduce to you, whichever the chairman prefers) Alderman_____ or City Councilman————or————, Alderman of the 5th District or————, City Councilman from the 5th District."

An ambassador is addressed in a letter as follows: His Excellency, the Ambassador of the French Republic to the United States of America, Washington, D. C. Sir:

(In place of Sir, it is also proper to use: Your Grace or Your Excellency.)

A letter addressed to the British Ambassador should read: His Excellency, His Britannic Majesty's Ambassador Extraordinary and Plenipotentiary at U. S. A., Washington, D. C. Dear Sir:

(Again it is proper and permissible to use, instead of Sir, Your Grace or Your Excellency.)

A chairman in introducing the Ambassador from France uses the term "His Excellency, the Ambassador of the French Republic to the United States of America." When introducing the British Ambassador, the chairman uses the term "His Excellency, His Brit-tanic Majesty's Ambassador Extraordinary and Plenipoteniary at U. S. A." All this, of course, after the usual preliminaries.

(194)

An Archbishop of the Anglican Church is addressed in a letter as follows:

His Grace, the Lord Archbishop of_____,

Church of_____,

Noport, N. Y.

My Lord Archbishop:

or

Your Grace:

The chairman in introducing the Archbishop refers to him as "The Lord Archbishop of_____" or "His Grace, The Lord Archbishop of_____."

A letter addressed to an Archbishop of the Roman Catholic church reads as follows:

His Grace, The Archbishop of ——————

or

The Most Reverend Archbishop of ————

or The Most Reverend Archbishop

The letter may be commenced: My Lord Archbishop:

or My Lord:

or Your Grace:

In addition, the term Most Reverend Sir or Most Reverend Archbishop may also be used in the letter.

A chairman in introducing the Archbishop of the Catholic Church may introduce him as The Lord Archbishop or His Grace, the Archbishop of_____, or The Most Reverend Archbishop of _____, or The Most Reverend Archbishop_____.

Other terms that may be used are: The Lord Archbishop

or

His Grace

or

The Most Reverend Archbishop

The terms set forth above are to be strictly adhered to. Modifications thereof are not permissible.

Army Officers are written to as follows: The Commander-in-Chief, Army of U. S. (Address)

Letters addressed to the Commander-in-Chief may commence: Sir:

Or

My dear General [which is very formal]:

or

Dear Commander:

Whenever a chairman introduces the Commander-in-Chief, he uses the term, "The Commander-in-Chief of the Army of the U. S." To an officer of lesser rank, the following is used in a letter:

Lt. General_____,

Commanding Officer, Army of U. S., (Address)

When introduced by a chairman the correct term is "Lt. General _____, Commanding _____."

If the letter is to go to a colonel, major, or captain, it should read as follows:

Colonel_____,

Commanding Officer of_____,

Army, U. S. A. (Address)

A chairman introduces a colonel as follows: "Colonel_____of _____Regiment, or Colonel of_____." The same for major or captain.

In addressing letters to army officers below the rank of captain,

(196)

the term Dear Mr._____, is used.
A chairman introduces a 1st lieutenant or 2nd lieutenant by using
the terms "1st Lieutenant_____now of_____." The same for
2nd lieutenant.

In writing to an assemblyman, the following form is used:
The Hon._____,
Member of the State Assembly, Albany, N. Y.
        or
Assemblyman_____,
Albany, N. Y.
              Letters commence: Sir:
        or
Dear Sir:
        or
My dear Mr._____:
The chairman introduces an assemblyman as follows: "The Hon.
_____, State Assemblyman, or_____, State Assembly
man from _____, District of_____."

To the Associate Justices of the Supreme Court of U. S., the
following is used:
The Hon._____, Associate Justice of Supreme Court of U. S.
        or
Honorable_____, Justice Supreme Court of U. S.
        or
Mr. Justice_____of Supreme Court of U. S.
              Letters commence:
Mr. Justice:
        or
Sir:
        or
Your Honor;

(197)

or

My Dear Mr. Justice:
The chairman introduces a judge of the Court as follows: "His
Honor_____Justice of Supreme Court of U. S., or Mr. Justice
_____of Supreme Court of U. S. Members of the bench are most
often introduced as His Honor,_____of_____ Court.

Bishop—(Anglican Church) :
The Right Reverend the Lord Bishop of————————

or

The Right Reverend Father in God
Letters commence: My Lord Bishop:

or

My Lord:
Bishop—(Methodist) :
Reverend Bishop _____
Letters commence:
Dear Sir:

or

Dear Bishop:

or

My dear Bishop:
Bishop—(Protestant Episcopal) :
Address:
To the Right Reverend_____, Bishop of _____
Letters commence:
Right Reverend and Dear Sir:

or

Dear Bishop:

or

My dear Bishop:
Bishop (Roman Catholic) :
The Lord Bishop of—————

or

(198)

His Lordship, the Bishop of ⎯⎯⎯⎯⎯
> *or*

The Most Reverend Bishop of _____
> Letters commence:

My Lord Bishop:

My Lord:
> *or*

Your Lordship:
> *or*

Your Excellency:

Bishop   (Scottish):
> The Right Reverend Bishop_____
> Letters commence:

Right Reverend Sir:

The chairman in all instances above, when it comes to introductions relating to members of the clergy, may use the designation in the letter, as for example, "The Right Reverend, the Lord Bishop of_____." Never use the pronoun "My" or "Your."

Cabinet Officers of U. S. A.:
> Address: The Hon. the Sec'y. of State (or Commerce or
Defense, etc.)
> *or*

The Hon. The Postmaster Gen.
> *or*

The Hon._____, Sec'y. of Interior (or State or Commerce, etc.)
> *or*

The Sec'y. of State (or Arty. Gen., etc.)
> Letters commence: Sir:
> *or*

Dear Sir:
> *or*

 My dear Mr. Sec'y. (Attorney General, etc.) :

Members of the Cabinet are introduced as "The Hon. ⎯⎯⎯⎯⎯

Sec'y· of State of U. S. of America," or "The Hon. _____, Post master General of U. S. A." etc.

Address a letter as follows: U. S. *or* The Chief Justice of the Supreme Court

or

The Hon. --------- , Chief Justice of the Supreme Court of the U. S.

Letters commence (to him alone) : Sir *or* Mr. Chief Justice:

or My dear Mr. Chief Justice:

or

(to him and his wife)
The Chief Justice and Mrs. ----------- :

Married Woman: Mrs. John Stout

Letters commence: Dear Madam:

or My dear Madam:

or My dear Mrs. Stout:

or

Dear Mrs. Stout: (most formal in case of a total stranger) Where lady is a widow her own first name is used: Mrs. Martha Stout.

A chairman in introducing a lady always uses the title Miss or Mrs. If the lady is married she is introduced as Mrs. John Stout; if she is a widow she is introduced as Mrs. Martha Stout. Where the lady is a public officer her title precedes her name, for example, "City Health Commissioner, Martha Stout" (whether married or not). Leave out Miss or Mrs. Her given first name is used.

(200)

Doctor of Divinity: Address:

Dr. ------------------

or

------------------ , D. D.

or

Rev. Dr. -------------------

Letters commence: Dear Sir: *or*

Mr dear Dr. ---------------------- :

or

Dear Dr. --------------------- :

or

Rev. Dr.:

The chairman may use any of the following terms in the introduction: Dr. Jonathan Johns or Reverend Dr. Jonathan Johns. Do not use other terms.

Governor:

Address:

His Excellency The Governor of -----------------

        or

His Excellency ------------------

        or

The Hon. the Governor of -------------------

        or

Hon. ------------------ , Governor of ----------

        Letters commence: Sir:

        or Dear Sir:

or

    My dear Mr. Governor: The chairman introduces the governor as "His Excellency John

Swift the Governor" or "His Excellency, Governor John Swift."

Judge:
Address:
The Hon. ------------------, U. S. District Judge for -------- Dist.
of ---------------------------- ,

       Letters commence: My dear Judge:
or
Dear Sir:
  A chairman introduces a judge as "His Honor Jock Jacques of
-------- , Conn, or Judge Jock Jacques of --------- , Conn.

Lawyer:
Address:
----------------- Esq. or Mr. --------- , Attorney at Law
or
Mr. ------------------, Attorney and Counsellor at Law
Letters commence:
Dear Sir *or* My Dear Mr.-------------------- :
  A chairman may introduce an attorney as either "Counsellor Hugh
Huff" or "Mr. Hugh Huff, Counsellor at Law."

Mayor:
Address:
The Hon. ------------------ , Mayor of ---------
     or
The Mayor of the City of --------------------
     Letters commence: Sir:
     or Dear Sir:
     or Dear Mr. Mayor:
or

My dear Mr. Mayor:

or

Dear Mayor:

    The chairman may use the terms: His Honor Oswald Waldorf, the Mayor; Mayor Oswald Waldorf; or Oswald Waldorf, the Mayor of the City of ---------- .

Naval Officers: Address:

The Admiral of the Navy of the U. S. *or*

      Admiral ------------------, Commanding U. S. Navy

      or

      Captain------------------ , U. S. N.

      Letters commence:

      Sir, or My dear Admiral, or Dear Captain ----------------- :

      For all officers below the rank of Captain:

      Dear Mr. ------------------:

    The chairman introduces the above officers in the same manner as the army officers above.

President of a college or university: Address:

    ---------------------------- Ll. D., Pres. of Univ. of ---------

    or

    Pres. ------------------of---------- University

        Letters commence: Dear Sir *or* Dear President:

    The chairman introduces the president of a university as "The President of--------- University,--------------------.

President of U. S.: Address: The President, The White House

    or

The President of U. S., The White House
       or His Excellency, The Pres. of U. S.
       Letters commence: Sir, *or* Mr. President:
A chairman introduces the President of U. S. as follows: "Ladies and Gentlemen, The President of the United States." Priest   (Roman Catholic) : Address:
The Rev. Father ------------------, O.S.M. (or other initials of his order)
Letters commence:
Rev. Father *or* Dear Father ------------------ :
The chairman introduces him as follows: "Father --------------- " or The Rev. ------------------ ."

Professor (in a college or university) :
Address:
Prof. ------------------
University of ------------------
-------------------------- , Prof, of history (mathematics, etc.)
Letters commence:
             Dear Sir, *or* My Dear Prof., *or* Dear Professor:
      A chairman introduces a professor as follows: "Professor John Quill of the Department of Botany of Forest University." If the professor is being introduced to a group at the university, he is introduced as "Professor John Quill of the Botany Department."

Rabbi:
Rabbi ----------------- , or Rev. -------- , or The Reverend -------- .
Letters commence:
Dear Sir, *or* Rev. Sir, *or* My dear Rabbi, *or* Dear Rabbi: *or*
    Dr. --------------------- (if he holds a doctor's degree) :
    A chairman introduces a Rabbi as "Rabbi ------------- of Temple or

Synagogue --------- or Dr. ---------- of ---------- Temple or Synagogue or Rev. Dr. ---------- of Temple or Synagogue ---------- (if the Rabbi is entitled to the title of "Doctor.")

Senator of the U. S.: Address:

The Hon. ------------------- , U. S. Senate,

Washington, D. C. *or*

Senator --------------------

Washington, D. C.

   Letters commence: Sir:

or

Dear Sir: *or* My dear Senator:

   or My dear Mr. Senator:

or

   Dear Senator: A senator is introduced by a chairman as follows: "The Hon.

--------, U. S. Senator from the State of -------------- . With slight modification a state senator is introduced in the above manner.

   A state senator is addressed and written to in the same manner as a U. S. senator.

BIBLIOGRAPHY

For those who are interested in studying more about these problems, here is a brief list of reference books.

Anderson, Virgil A., *Training the Speaking Voice* (Oxford University Press, 1942)

Carnegie, Dale, *Public Speaking and Influencing Men in Business* (Association Press, 1943)

Cushing, Luther Stearns, *Cusking's Manual of Parliamentary Practice* (Winston, 1947)

Eastman, Max, *The Enjoyment of Laughter* (Simon and Schuster, 1936)

Ewbank, H. L, and Auer, J. J., *Discussion and Debate* (Crofts, 1941)

Hanna, Mark, *Public Speaking without Fear and Trembling* (Macmillan, 1949)

Hayakawa, S., *Language in Action* (Harcourt, Brace, 1941)

Henry, William H. F., and Seeley, Levi, *How to Organize and Conduct a Meeting* (Noble and Noble, 1938)

Hollingsworth, H. L., *The Psychology of the Audience* (American Book Company, 1935)

Howe, F. W., *Handbook of Parliamentary Usage* (Noble and Noble)

Hunt, Edward E., *Conferences, Committees, Conventions, and How to Run Them* (Harper, 1925)

Jones, Edgar De Witt, *The Lords of Speech* (Willett, Clark, 1937)

Karr, Harrison M., *Your Speaking Voice* (Glendale Printers, Glendale, California, 1938)

Laguna, Grace Andrus de, *Speech: Its Function and Development* (Yale University Press, 1927)

Lomas, Charles W., "The Psychology of Stage Fright," in *The Quarterly Journal of Speech,* XXIII (February, 1937)

McBurney, J. H., and Hance, K. G., *The Principles and Methods of Discussion* (Harper, 1939)

McBurney, J. H., and Hance, K. G., *Discussion in Human Affairs* (Harper, 1950)

McCall, Roy C, *Fundamentals of Speech* (Macmillan, 1949)

Monroe, Alan H., *Principles and Types of Speech* (Scott, Foresman, 1939)

Moore, Zoe Steen, and Moore, John B., *Essentials of Parliamentary Procedure* (Harper, 1944)

Nizer, Louis, *Thinking on Your Feet* (Liveright, 1940)

Oliver, Robert T., and Cortright, Rupert T., *The New Training for Effective Speech* (revised edition, Dryden Press, 1950)

Oliver, R. T., Dickey, D. C, and Zelko, H. P., *Essentials of Communicative Speech* (Dryden Press, 1949)

O'Neill, James M., Laycock, Craven, and Scales, Robert L., *Argumentation and Debate* (Macmillan, 1928)

(207)

HOW TO PLAN MEETINGS

Robert, H. M., *Rules of Order* (revised edition, Scott, 1943)

Robbins, H. W., and Oliver, R. T., *Developing Ideas* (Longmans, Green, 1943)

Sarett, Lew, and Foster, William T., *Basic Principles of Speech* (Houghton, Mifflin, 1946)

Watkins, Dwight E., and Karr, Harrison M., *Stage Fright and What To Do About It* (Expression Company, 1940)

West, Robert, *Purposive Speaking* (Macmillan, 1925)

Wiese, Mildred, Bryson, Lyman, and Hallenbeck, W. C, *Let's Talk It Over* (University of Chicago Press, 1936)

Wines, Emma M., and Card, M. W.₃ *"Come to Order!"* (Doubleday, Do-ran, 1929)

Also available from www.sunvillagepublications.com

BRAIN STORMING
The Dynamic Way To Create Successful New Ideas

Charles H. Clark

How To Write SUCCESSFUL BUSINESS LETTERS In Just 15 Days

John P. Riebel

CHALK TALK MADE EASY
A COMPLETE SELF-INSTRUCTION COURSE IN CRAYON AND BLACKBOARD DRAWING

BY WILLIAM ALLEN BIXLER "THE RILEY ARTIST"

USING CHARTS TO IMPROVE PROFITS

Ely Francis

How To Help Groups Make Decisions

Grace Loucks Elliott

HOW TO CREATE NEW IDEAS
A Comprehensive Course In The Art and Science of Creative Thinking

Jack W. Taylor

How To Plan Meetings
And Be A Successful Chairperson

Joseph G. Glass, PH.B., LL.B.

How To Run BETTER MEETINGS

Edward J. Hegarty

The Successful Sales Meetings Handbook
Bill N. Newman